Jacob's Ladder
Reading Comprehension Program

Second Edition

Grade 4

Jacob's Ladder
Reading Comprehension Program

Second Edition

Grade 4

Contributing Editors:

Joyce VanTassel-Baska, Tamra Stambaugh, Kimberley L. Chandler

Contributing Authors:

Heather French, Paula Ginsburgh, Tamra Stambaugh, Joyce VanTassel-Baska

William & Mary
School of Education
CENTER FOR GIFTED EDUCATION

William & Mary
School of Education
Center for Gifted Education
P.O. Box 8795
Williamsburg, VA 23187

Copyright ©2018, Center for Gifted Education, William & Mary

Edited by Lacy Compton

Cover design by Raquel Trevino and layout design by Allegra Denbo

ISBN-13: 978-1-61821-714-1

No part of this book may be reproduced, translated, stored in a retrieval system, or transmitted, in any form or by any means, electronic, mechanical, photocopying, microfilming, recording, or otherwise, without written permission from the publisher.

Prufrock Press grants the individual purchasing this book permission to photocopy original activity pages for single classroom use. This permission does not include electronic reproduction rights. Should you wish to make copies of materials we sourced or licensed from others, request permission from the original publisher before reproducing that material.

For more information about our copyright policy or to request reprint permissions, visit https://www.prufrock.com/permissions.aspx.

Printed in the United States of America.

At the time of this book's publication, all facts and figures cited are the most current available. All telephone numbers, addresses, and website URLs are accurate and active. All publications, organizations, websites, and other resources exist as described in the book, and all have been verified. The author and Prufrock Press Inc. make no warranty or guarantee concerning the information and materials given out by organizations or content found at websites, and we are not responsible for any changes that occur after this book's publication. If you find an error, please contact Prufrock Press Inc.

Prufrock Press Inc.
P.O. Box 8813
Waco, TX 76714-8813
Phone: (800) 998-2208
Fax: (800) 240-0333
http://www.prufrock.com

Table of Contents

Part I: Teachers' Guide to Jacob's Ladder
Reading Comprehension Program 1

Part II: Readings and Student Ladder Sets 19
    Chapter 1: Short Stories 21
    Chapter 2: Poetry 61
    Chapter 3: Nonfiction 91

Appendix A: Pre- and Postassessments
and Exemplars 119

Appendix B: Record-Keeping Forms/Documents 135

Answer Key 145

Common Core State Standards Alignment 167

Part I: Teachers' Guide to Jacob's Ladder Reading Comprehension Program

Introduction to *Jacob's Ladder, Grade 4*

Jacob's Ladder, Grade 4 (2nd ed.) is a supplemental reading program that implements targeted readings from short stories, poetry, and nonfiction sources, building on the work in the previous edition, *Jacob's Ladder, Level 2*. With this program, students engage in an inquiry process that moves from lower order to higher order thinking skills. Starting with basic literary understanding, students learn to analyze texts critically by determining implications and consequences, generalizations, main ideas, and/or creative synthesis. Suggested for students in grade 4 to enhance reading comprehension and critical thinking, *Jacob's Ladder, Grade 4* tasks are organized into four skill ladders: A–D. Each ladder focuses on a different skill. Students "climb" each ladder by answering lower level questions before moving to higher level questions or rungs at the top of each ladder. Each ladder stands alone and focuses on a separate critical thinking component in reading.

Ladder A focuses on implications and consequences. By leading students through sequencing and cause-and-effect activities, students learn to draw implications and consequences from readings. Ladder B focuses on making generalizations. Students first learn to provide details and examples, then move to classifying and organizing those details in order to make generalizations. Ladder C focuses on main ideas, themes, or concepts. Students begin by identifying setting and characters and then make inferences about the literary situation. Ladder D focuses on creative synthesis by leading students through paraphrasing and summarizing activities. Table 1 provides a visual representation of the four ladders and corresponding objectives for each ladder and rung.

The second editions in the *Jacob's Ladder* series consist of seven levels, divided by grade: K–1, 1–2, 3, 4, 5, 6–7, and 7–8. Most of the books contain short stories, poetry, and nonfiction selections, including biographies. Additionally, most of the pieces include at least two commensurate ladders for each selection, with a few exceptions (e.g., the K–1 poetry section and the Level 1 poetry section, which have one ladder per poem). *Jacob's Ladder, K–1* and *1–2* differ from the rest of the series in that the majority of the short stories are Caldecott Medal or Caldecott Honor picture books. Many of the stories are intended to be read aloud for the first reading. In addition, although *Jacob's Ladder, K–1* does contain poetry, it does not contain nonfiction selections.

Although grade-level distinctions have been set for each of the second editions, teachers may find that they want to vary usage beyond the recommended levels, depending on student abilities. Evidence suggests that the curriculum can be successfully implemented with gifted learners and advanced readers, as well as promising learners, at different grade levels. Thus, the levels vary and overlap to provide opportunities for teachers to select the most appropriate set of readings for meaningful differentiation for their gifted, bright, or promising learners.

Ladder A: Focus on Implications and Consequences

The goal of Ladder A is to develop prediction and forecasting skills by encouraging students to make connections among the information provided. Starting with sequencing, students learn to recognize basic types of change that occur within a text. Through identifying cause-and-effect relationships, students then can judge the impact of certain events. Finally, through recognizing consequences and implications, students predict future events as logical and identify both short- and long-term consequences by judging probable outcomes based on data provided. The rungs are as follows:

- **Ladder A, Rung 1, Sequencing**: The lowest rung on the ladder, sequencing, requires students to organize a set of information in order, based on their reading (e.g., List the steps of a recipe in order).

TABLE 1
Goals and Objectives of Jacob's Ladder by Ladder and Rung

Ladder A	Ladder B	Ladder C	Ladder D
A3: Consequences and Implications — Students will be able to predict character actions, story outcomes, and make real-world forecasts.	**B3: Generalizations** — Students will be able to make general statements about a reading and/or an idea within the reading, using data to support their statements.	**C3: Main Idea, Theme, or Concept** — Students will be able to identify a major idea, theme, or concept common throughout the text.	**D3: Creative Synthesis** — Students will create something new using what they have learned from the reading and their synopses.
A2: Cause and Effect — Students will be able to identify and predict relationships between character behavior and story events, and their effects upon other characters or events.	**B2: Classifications** — Students will be able to categorize different aspects of the text or identify and sort categories from a list of topics or details.	**C2: Inference** — Students will be able to use textual clues to read between the lines and make judgments about specific textual events, ideas, or character analysis.	**D2: Summarizing** — Students will be able to provide a synopsis of text sections.
A1: Sequencing — Students will be able to list, in order of importance or occurrence in the text, specific events or plot summaries.	**B1: Details** — Students will be able to list specific details or recall facts related to the text or generate a list of ideas about a specific topic or character.	**C1: Literary Elements** — Students will be able to identify and explain specific story elements, such as character, setting, or poetic device.	**D1: Paraphrasing** — Students will be able to restate lines read using their own words.

Teachers' Guide

- **Ladder A, Rung 2, Cause and Effect**: The middle rung, cause and effect, requires students to think about relationships and identify what causes certain effects and/or what effects were brought about because of certain causes (e.g., What causes a cake to rise in the oven? What effect does the addition of egg yolks have on a batter?).

- **Ladder A, Rung 3, Consequences and Implications**: The highest rung on Ladder A requires students to think about both short-term and long-term events that may happen as a result of an effect they have identified (e.g., What are the short-term and long-term consequences of not saving any money?). Students learn to see implications and determine consequences from text for application in the real world. An implication is a possible result of an action. A consequence is the actual result of an action.

Ladder B: Focus on Generalizations

The goal of Ladder B is to help students develop deductive reasoning skills, moving from the concrete elements in a story to abstract ideas. Students begin by learning the importance of concrete details and how they can be organized. By the top rung, students are able to make general statements spanning a topic or concept. The rungs are as follows:

- **Ladder B, Rung 1, Details**: The lowest rung on Ladder B, details, requires students to list examples or details from what they have read and/or to list examples they know from the real world or have read about (e.g., Make a list of examples of transportation. Write as many as you can think of in 2 minutes).

- **Ladder B, Rung 2, Classifications**: The middle rung of Ladder B focuses on students' ability to categorize examples and details based on characteristics (e.g., How might we categorize the modes of transportation you identified?). This activity builds students' skills in categorization and classification.

- **Ladder B, Rung 3, Generalizations**: The highest rung on Ladder B, generalizations, requires students to use the list and categories generated at Rungs 1 and 2 to develop 2–3 general statements that apply to *all* of their examples (e.g., Write three statements about transportation).

This ladder is based on the Taba Model of Concept Development. Hilda Taba's Concept Development model (Taba, 1962) involves both inductive and deductive reasoning processes.

The model includes the following steps:

1. Begin with a broad concept, such as *change, conflict,* or *system.*
2. List as many examples of the concept as possible.
3. Categorize the examples to determine connections and to organize ideas.
4. Think of nonexamples of the concept.
5. Develop generalizations about the concept. Generalizations are universal statements about the concept. They are abstract and high level in nature.

Ladder C: Focus on Main Ideas, Themes, or Concepts

The goal of Ladder C is to develop literary analysis skills based on an understanding of literary elements. After completing Ladder C, students may state the main idea, the theme, or the overarching concept of a text after identifying setting, characters, and the context of the piece. The rungs are as follows:

- **Ladder C, Rung 1, Literary Elements**: While working on Rung 1, students identify and/or describe the setting or situation in which the reading occurs. This rung also requires students to develop an understanding of a given character by identifying qualities he or she possesses and comparing these qualities to other characters they have encountered in their reading (e.g., In *Goldilocks and the Three Bears*, what is the situation in which Goldilocks finds herself? What qualities do you admire in Goldilocks? What qualities do you find problematic? How is she similar to or different from other fairy tale characters you have encountered?).

- **Ladder C, Rung 2, Inference**: Inference serves as the middle rung of this ladder and requires students to think through a situation in the text and come to a conclusion based on the information and clues provided (e.g., What evidence exists that Goldilocks ate the porridge? What inferences can you make about the bear's subsequent action?).

- **Ladder C, Rung 3, Main Idea, Theme, or Concept**: As the highest rung of Ladder C, this step requires students to state the main idea, theme, or overarching concept for a reading. This exercise may ask students to explain an idea from the reading that best states what the text means (e.g., How would you rename the fairy tale? Why? What is the overall theme of *Goldilocks and the Three Bears*? Which of the following morals apply to the fairy tale? Why or why not?). This exercise also may require students to identify the overarching concept in a selection.

Ladder D: Focus on Creative Synthesis

The goal of Ladder D is to help students develop skills in creative synthesis in order to foster students' creation of new material based on information from the reading. It moves from the level of restating ideas to creating new ideas about a topic or concept. The rungs are as follows:

- **Ladder D, Rung 1, Paraphrasing**: The lowest rung on Ladder D is paraphrasing. This rung requires students to restate a short passage using their own words (e.g., Rewrite the following quotation in your own words: "But as soon as [the Lion] came near to Androcles, he recognized his friend, and fawned upon him, and licked his hands like a friendly dog. The emperor, surprised at this, summoned Androcles to him, who told the whole story. Whereupon the slave was pardoned and freed, and the Lion let loose to his native forest.").

- **Ladder D, Rung 2, Summarizing**: Summarizing, the middle rung, requires students to summarize larger sections of text by selecting the most important key points within a passage (e.g., Choose one section of the story and summarize it in five sentences).

- **Ladder D, Rung 3, Creative Synthesis**: The highest rung on Ladder D requires students to create something new using what they have learned from the reading and their synopses of it (e.g., Write another fable about the main idea you identified for this fable, using characters, setting, and a plot of your choice).

Process Skills

Along with the four goals addressed by the ladders, a fifth goal, process skills, is incorporated in the *Jacob's Ladder* curriculum. The aim of this goal is to promote learning through interaction and discussion of reading material in the classroom. After completing the ladders and following guidelines for discussion and teacher feedback, students will be able to:

- articulate their understanding of a reading passage using textual support,
- engage in proper dialogue about the meaning of a selection, and
- discuss varied ideas about intention of a passage both orally and in writing.

Reading Genres and Selections

The reading selections include three major genres: short stories (fables, myths, short stories, and essays), poetry, and nonfiction. In the grade 4 book, each reading within a genre has been carefully selected or tailored for fourth-grade reading accessibility and interest. The stories and poems for the *Jacob's Ladder* curriculum at each grade level were chosen with three basic criteria in mind: (1) concrete to abstract development, (2) level of vocabulary, and (3) age-appropriate themes. The readings and exercises are designed to move students forward in their abstract thinking processes by promoting critical and creative thinking. The vocabulary in each reading is grade-level appropriate; however, when new or unfamiliar words are encountered, they should be covered in class before readings and ladder questions are assigned. Themes also are appropriate to the students' ages at each grade level and were chosen to complement themes typically seen in texts for each particular level. The short stories, poetry, and nonfiction readings with corresponding ladder sets are delineated in Part II. Table 2 outlines all grade 4 readings by genre.

Rationale

Constructing meaning of the written word is one of the earliest tasks required of students in schools. This skill occupies the central place in the curriculum at the elementary level. Yet, approaches to teaching reading comprehension often are "skill and drill," using worksheets on low-level reading material. As a result, students frequently are unable to transfer these skills from exercise pages and apply them to new higher level reading material.

The time expended to ensure that students become autonomous and advanced readers would suggest the need for a methodology that deliberately moves students from simple to complex reading skills with grade-

TABLE 2
Reading Selections by Genre

Short Stories	Poetry	Nonfiction
Androcles	I Am Autumn	The American Revolutionary War
Arachne and Athena	13 Ways of Looking at a Rose	The Exploration of Space
Rumpel-Stilts-Ken	Sweet Summer	Graphic Ice Cream
The Three Painters	My Shadow	The Great Depression
The Fox and the Cat	After the Winter	It's Electric!
The Lost Wig	Travel	The Metric System vs. The U.S. Customary System
Finding the Writer Inside	Saving Words	
The Myth of Athena	Dubstep	
The Myth of Heracles (Hercules)	Approach of Winter	
Theseus and the Minotaur		

appropriate texts. Such a learning approach to reading skill development ensures that students can traverse easily from basic comprehension skills to higher level critical reading skills, while using the same reading stimulus to navigate this transition. Reading comprehension is enhanced by instructional scaffolding, moving students from lower order to higher order thinking, using strategies and processes to help students analyze passages (Fisher & Frey, 2014; Peterson & Taylor, 2012). In addition, teachers who emphasize higher order thinking through questions and tasks such as those at the higher rungs of each ladder promote greater reading growth (Degener & Berne, 2016). *Jacob's Ladder* was written in response to teacher findings that students needed additional scaffolding to work consistently at higher levels of thinking in reading.

In addition, the adoption of the Common Core State Standards (CCSS) in 2010, or state standards that mimicked the CCSS, resulted in a new emphasis on the close reading of complex text. This involves making annotations, using text-dependent questions, and holding discussions about texts. Harvey and Goudvis (2007) have promoted the use of text coding and annotating as methods for students to deepen comprehension. In order to focus students' attention on specific elements of text in multiple readings, researchers have emphasized the need for teachers to provide text-dependent questions (Fisher & Frey, 2012; Lapp, Grant, Moss, & Johnson, 2013; Santori & Belfatti, 2017). Text-based discussion can facilitate reading comprehension by allowing students to construct their understanding of ideas in collaboration with their classmates (DeFrance & Fahrenbruck, 2015). Researchers have also noted the importance of discussions for enhancing student talk about texts and improving the comprehension of text (Duke, Pearson, Strachan, & Billman, 2011; Lawrence & Snow, 2011). Most of the questions in *Jacob's Ladder* are text-dependent questions. Discussions may be done in dyads, small groups, or with the entire class. Although *Jacob's Ladder* does not specifically address text coding or annotating, those are strategies that could easily be incorporated as students read the selections.

The *Jacob's Ladder* program is a compilation of the instructional scaffolding and reading exercises necessary to aid students in their journey toward becoming critical readers. Students learn concept development skills through learning to generalize, predicting and forecasting skills through delineating implications of events, and literary analysis skills through discerning textual meaning. The questions and tasks for each reading are open-ended, as this type of approach to responding to literature improves performance on comprehension tests (Wasik & Hindman, 2013). Progressing through the hierarchy of skills also requires students to reread the text, thereby improving metacomprehension accuracy (Hedin & Conderman, 2010).

Research Base

A quasi-experimental study was conducted using *Jacob's Ladder* as a supplementary program for students in Title I schools, grades 3–5. After professional development occurred, experimental teachers were instructed to implement the *Jacob's Ladder* curriculum in addition to their basal reading series and guided reading groups. Teachers in the control group taught their district-adopted textbook reading series as the main curriculum.

Findings from this study ($N = 495$) suggest that when compared to students who used the basal reader only, those students who were exposed to the *Jacob's Ladder* curriculum showed significant gains in reading comprehension and critical thinking. Likewise, students who used the curriculum showed significant and important growth on curriculum-based assessments that included determining implications/consequences, making inferences, outlining themes and generalizations, and applying creative synthesis. Students reported greater interest in reading and alluded that the curriculum made them "think harder." Teachers reported more in-depth student discussion and personal growth in the ability to ask open-ended questions when reading (Stambaugh, 2007).

Implementation Considerations

Teachers need to consider certain issues when implementing the *Jacob's Ladder* curriculum. Although the program is targeted for promising students who need more exposure to higher level thinking skills in reading, the program may be suitable for learners who are functioning above or below grade level.

As modeling, coaching, and feedback appear to enhance student growth in reading and writing (Fisher & Frey, 2015), it is recommended that teachers review how to complete the task ladders with the entire class at least once, outlining expectations and record-keeping tasks, as well as modeling the process prior to assigning small-group or independent work. Students should complete the ladder tasks on their own paper or on the template provided in Appendix B. As students gain more confidence in the curriculum, the teacher should allow more independent work coupled with small-group or paired discussion, and then whole-group sharing with teacher feedback.

Completing these activities in dyads or small groups will facilitate discussions that stress collaborative reasoning, thereby fostering greater engagement and higher level thinking (Duke et al., 2011; Lawrence & Snow, 2011). The stories and accompanying ladder questions and activities also may be organized into a reading center in the classroom or utilized with reading groups during guided reading.

Process of Jacob's Ladder

The process of inquiry and feedback, as led and modeled by the teacher, is critical to the success of the program and student mastery of process skills. Teachers need to encourage and solicit multiple student responses and encourage dialogue about various perspectives and interpretations of a given text, requiring students to justify their answers with textual support and concrete examples. Student use of the ladders depends on teacher stance and modeling as well as student readiness. After teacher modeling, students should understand how to use the ladders as prescribed by the teacher. Sample follow-up questions such as those listed below can be used by the teacher and posted in the classroom to help guide student discussion.

- That's interesting; does anyone have a different idea?
- What in the story makes you say that?

- What do you think the author means by . . . ?
- What do you think are the implications or consequences of . . . ?
- Did anyone view that differently? How?
- Does anyone have a different point of view? Justify your answer.
- In the story I noticed that . . . Do you think that might have significance to the overall meaning?
- I heard someone say that he thought the poem (story) was about . . . What do you think? Justify your answer from the events of the story.
- Do you notice any key words that might be significant? Why?
- Do you notice any words that give you a mental picture? Do those words have significance? What might they symbolize?
- I agree with . . . because . . .
- I had a different idea than . . . because . . .

Grouping Students

Jacob's Ladder may be used in a number of different grouping patterns. The program should be introduced initially as a whole-group activity directed by the teacher with appropriate open-ended questions, feedback, and monitoring. After students have examined each type of ladder with teacher guidance, they should be encouraged to use the program by writing ideas independently, sharing with a partner, and then discussing the findings with a group. The dyad approach provides maximum opportunities for student discussion of the readings and collaborative decisions about the answers to questions posed. One purpose of the program is to solicit meaningful discussion of the text. Like-ability groups are recommended (Kulik & Kulik, 1992) for discussion.

Pre- and Postassessments and Grading

The pre- and postassessments included in Appendix A were designed as a diagnostic-prescriptive approach to guide program implementation prior to the implementation of *Jacob's Ladder*. The pretest should be administered, scored, and then used to guide student instruction and the selection of readings for varied ability groups. Both the pre- and postassessment, scoring rubric, and sample exemplars for each rubric category and level are included in Appendix A along with exemplars to guide scoring.

In both the pre- and postassessments, students read a short passage and respond to the four questions. Question 1 focuses on implications and consequences (Ladder A); Question 2 on inference (Ladder C); Question 3 on generalization, theme, and concept (Ladders B and C); and Question 4 on creative synthesis (Ladder D). By analyzing each question and scored response, teachers may wish to guide reading selections toward the appropriate ladders and stories based on student need.

Upon conclusion of the program or as a midpoint check, the posttest may be administered to compare the pretest results and to measure growth in students' responses. These pre/post results could be used as part of a student portfolio, in a parent-teacher conference, or documentation of curriculum effectiveness and student progress. The pre- and postassessments were piloted to ensure that both forms were equivalent in difficulty (a = .76) and that the interrater reliability of scorers was appropriate (a = .81).

Student Reflection, Feedback, and Record Keeping

Students may use the Brainstorming/Answer sheet provided in Appendix B for each ladder to record their personal thoughts independently before discussing with a partner. After finishing both of the ladders for each reading selection, a reflection page, My Reflection on Today's Reading and Discussion (also in Appendix B), can be provided, indicating the student's personal assessment of the work completed. Teachers also will want to check student answers as ladder segments are completed and conduct an error analysis. Individual or small-group consultation should occur at this time to ensure that students understand what they did incorrectly and why. In order to analyze student responses and progress across the program, teachers need to monitor student performance, using the student answer sheets to indicate appropriate completion of tasks. Specific comments about student work also are important to promote growth and understanding of content.

The Assessment/Response Form (Appendix B) may be used by the student as an answer sheet for a given ladder. The student may self-assess his or her work on the ladder in the form of a numerical score. The teacher may also provide a numerical score for feedback. In addition, there is space for both the student and the teacher to write comments about the student's work on the ladder.

Classroom Diagnostic Forms also are provided in Appendix B. On these forms, teachers record student progress on a 3-point scale: 2 (*exceeds expectations; applies skills very effectively*), 1 (*satisfactory; understands and applies skills*), or a 0 (*needs improvement; needs more practice with the given skill set*) across readings and ladder sets. These forms can be used as part of a diagnostic-prescriptive approach to selecting reading materials and ladders based on student understanding or the need for more practice.

Sample Concluding Activities

Grading the ladders and responses is at the teacher's discretion. Many teachers use *Jacob's Ladder* for practice purposes only and do not grade them. As students initially learn how to complete *Jacob's Ladder* activities, teachers should provide feedback about their work, but not grades. If the teacher eventually decides to assign grades after students understand what to do, he or she should not overemphasize the lower rungs in graded activities. Lower rungs are intended only as a vehicle to the higher level questions at the top of the ladder. Instead, top rung questions may be used as a journal prompt or as part of a graded open-ended writing response. Grades also could be given based on guided discussion after students are trained on appropriate ways to discuss literature. Additional ideas for grading are as follows:

- Write a persuasive essay to justify what you think the story is about.
- Create a symbol to show the meaning of the story. Write two sentences to justify your answer.
- In one word or phrase, what is this story mostly about? Justify your answer using examples from the story.
- Write a letter from the author's point of view, explaining what the meaning of the story is to young children.
- Pretend you are an illustrator. Create a drawing for the story or poem that shows the main idea or theme. Write a sentence that describes your illustration and theme.

Time Allotment

Although the time needed to complete *Jacob's Ladder* tasks will vary by student, most ladders should take students 15 minutes to read the selection and another 20–30 minutes to complete one ladder individually. More time is required for paired student and whole-group discussion of the questions. Teachers may wish to set aside 2 days each week for focusing on one *Jacob's Ladder* reading and the two commensurate ladders, especially when introducing the program.

Answer Key

An answer key is included at the end of the book. It contains a set of suggested answers for all questions related to each reading selection. All of the questions are somewhat open-ended; therefore, answers may vary. The answers provided in the key are simply suggestions to help illustrate the skills targeted by each ladder skill set.

Alignment to Standards

Tables 3, 4, and 5 contain alignment charts to demonstrate the connection of the fiction and nonfiction reading materials to relevant national standards in all subject areas. One of the benefits of this program is its ability to provide cross-disciplinary coverage of standards through the use of a single reading stimulus.

TABLE 3
Standards Alignment: Short Stories

Language Arts—Short Stories	Androcles	Arachne and Athena	Rumpel-Stilts-Ken	The Three Painters	The Fox and the Cat	The Lost Wig	Finding the Writer Inside	The Myth of Athena	The Myth of Heracles (Hercules)	Theseus and the Minotaur
The student will use analysis of text, including the interaction of the text with a reader's feelings and attitudes to create a response.		✗				✗		✗		
The student will interpret and analyze the meaning of literary works from diverse cultures and authors by applying different critical lenses and analytic techniques.	✗	✗	✗	✗	✗	✗	✗	✗	✗	
The student will integrate various cues and strategies to comprehend what he or she reads.	✗	✗	✗	✗	✗	✗	✗	✗	✗	✗
The student will use knowledge of the purposes, structures, and elements of writing to analyze and interpret various types of text.	✗	✗	✗	✗	✗	✗	✗	✗	✗	✗
Students will use word-analysis skills, context clues, and other strategies to read fiction and non-fiction with fluency and accuracy.	✗	✗	✗	✗	✗	✗	✗	✗	✗	✗

TABLE 4
Standards Alignment: Poetry

Language Arts—Poetry	I Am Autumn	13 Ways of Looking at a Rose	Sweet Summer	My Shadow	After the Winter	Travel	Saving Words	Dubstep	Approach of Winter
The student will use analysis of text, including the interaction of the text with a reader's feelings and attitudes to create a response.	X	X	X	X	X	X	X	X	X
The student will interpret and analyze the meaning of literary works from diverse cultures and authors by applying different critical lenses and analytic techniques.	X	X	X	X	X	X		X	X
The student will integrate various cues and strategies to comprehend what he or she reads.	X	X	X	X	X	X	X		X
The student will use knowledge of the purposes, structures, and elements of writing to analyze and interpret various types of text.	X	X		X	X		X	X	X

TABLE 5
Standards Alignment: Nonfiction

Social Studies, Science, and Math Standards	The American Revolutionary War	The Exploration of Space	Graphic Ice Cream	The Great Depression	It's Electric!	The Metric System vs. The U.S. Customary System
Social Studies Standards						
Culture	✗			✗		
Time, Continuity, and Change	✗			✗		
People, Places, and Environments						
Individual Development and Identity						
Individuals, Groups, and Institutions	✗			✗		
Science, Technology, and Society						
Science Standards						
Science as Inquiry		✗				
Physical Science		✗			✗	
Life Science						
Earth and Space Science		✗				
Science and Technology		✗			✗	
Science in Personal and Social Perspective						
History and Nature of Science					✗	
Math Standards						
Number and Operations						✗
Geometry						
Measurement			✗			✗
Data Analysis and Probability			✗			
Problem Solving						
Communication						
Connections						

Teachers' Guide 17

References

DeFrance, N. L., Fahrenbruck, M. L. (2015). Constructing a plan for text-based discussion. *Journal of Adolescent & Adult Literacy, 59,* 575–585. doi:10.1002/jaal.477

Degener, S., & Berne, J. (2016). Complex questions promote complex thinking. *The Reading Teacher, 70,* 595–599. doi:10.1002/trtr.1535

Duke, N. K., Pearson, P. D., Strachan, S. L., & Billman, A. K. (2011). Essential elements of fostering and teaching reading comprehension. In S. J. Samuels & A. E. Farstrup (Eds.), *What research has to say about reading instruction* (pp. 51–93). Newark, DE: International Reading Association. doi:10.1598/0829.03

Fisher, D., & Frey, N. (2012). Close reading in elementary schools. *The Reading Teacher, 66,* 179–188. doi:10.1002/TRTR.01117

Fisher, D., & Frey, N. (2014). Scaffolded reading instruction of content-area texts. *The Reading Teacher, 67,* 347–351. doi:10.1002/trtr.1234

Fisher, D., & Frey, N. (2015). Teacher modeling using complex informational texts. *The Reading Teacher, 69*(1), 63–69. doi:10.1002/trtr.1372

Harvey, S., & Goudvis, A. (2007). *Strategies that work: Teaching comprehension for understanding and engagement* (2nd ed.). Portland, ME: Stenhouse Publishers.

Hedin, L. R., & Conderman, G. (2010). Teaching students to comprehend informational text through rereading. *The Reading Teacher, 63,* 556–565. doi:10.1598/RT.63.7.3

Kulik, J. A., & Kulik, C.-L. C. (1992). Meta-analytic findings on grouping programs. *Gifted Child Quarterly, 36,* 73–77.

Lapp, D., Grant, M., Moss, B., & Johnson, K. (2013). Close reading of science texts: What's now? What's next? *The Reading Teacher, 67,* 109–119.

Lawrence, J. F., & Snow, C. E. (2011). Oral discourse and reading. In M. L. Kamil, P. D. Pearson, E. B. Moje, & P. P. Afflerbach (Eds.), *Handbook of reading research* (Vol. 4, pp. 320–337). New York, NY: Routledge.

Peterson, D. S., & Taylor, B. M. (2012). Using higher order questioning to accelerate students' growth in reading. *The Reading Teacher, 65,* 295–304. doi:10.1002/TRTR.01045

Santori, D., & Belfatti, M. (2017). Do text-dependent questions need to be teacher-dependent? Close reading from another angle. *The Reading Teacher, 70,* 649–657. doi:10.1002/trtr.1555

Stambaugh, T. (2007). *Effects of the Jacob's Ladder Reading Comprehension Program* (Unpublished doctoral dissertation). William & Mary, Williamsburg, VA.

Taba, H. (1962). *Curriculum development: Theory and practice.* New York, NY: Harcourt, Brace & World.

Wasik, B. A., & Hindman, A. H. (2013). Realizing the promise of open-ended questions. *The Reading Teacher, 67,* 302–311. doi:10.1002/trtr.1218

Part II: Readings and Student Ladder Sets

Chapter 1: Short Stories and Corresponding Ladders
Chapter 2: Poetry and Corresponding Ladders
Chapter 3: Nonfiction and Corresponding Ladders

Name: _____ Date: _____

Arachne and Athena

Arachne, who lived in Greece during ancient times, was famous for her incredible talent in weaving cloth. She could make the most beautiful cloth in the entire land. However, Arachne was not a modest girl. She would walk through the city boasting about her incredible talents. Arachne would even tell people that she was better at weaving than the revered goddess Athena.

Athena was not pleased by Arachne's boasting. One day, Athena knocked on Arachne's door. Arachne opened the door to find an old lady dressed in ragged clothes. She did not know she was really looking at Athena in disguise. The old lady pretended to be interested in buying some of Arachne's cloth. Arachne let the old lady enter. Immediately, Athena, disguised as the old lady, started criticizing Arachne's weaving, saying she could do much better. Insulted, Arachne challenged the old lady to a weaving contest.

After accepting the challenge, Athena emerged from her disguise. Arachne was not at all frightened by the prospect of a weaving competition with Athena; Arachne was completely convinced she would win!

Both Arachne and Athena spent hours weaving beautiful cloth. Athena's cloth was spectacular. She had woven a picture of the gods performing their many wonderful deeds. Arachne's cloth also portrayed the gods and was equally stunning. However, Arachne's cloth portrayed the gods at their weakest moments, displaying their worst behavior. Athena was furious. She could not believe Arachne had the audacity to insult the gods.

Athena complimented Arachne on her amazing weaving talent and told her she would be justly rewarded for her gifts. Arachne felt her head begin to shrink and watched in horror as eight furry legs sprouted from her body. Athena told her to enjoy spending the rest of her days weaving all she wished.

Short Stories

Name: _____ Date: _____

Generalizations

B3

What generalizations can you make about change based on your list and categories?

Classifications

B2

Using the list you created in B1, categorize the changes you listed.

Details

B1

List 25 ways Arachne's life might change now that she is a spider.

ARACHNE AND ATHENA

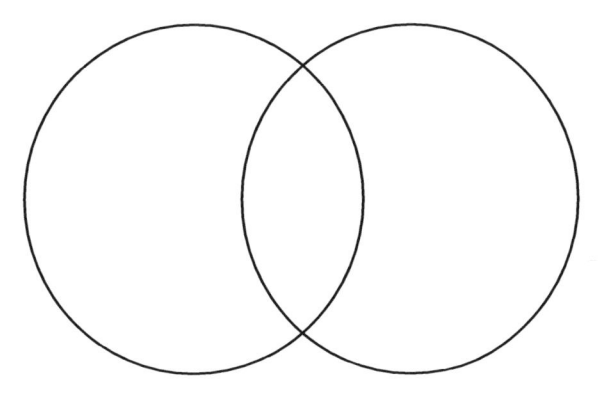

Name: _____ Date: _____

Main Idea, Theme, or Concept

C3

Theme: What moral could we learn from this myth? Support your answer with evidence from the text.

Inference

C2

Why did Arachne try to out-weave Athena? What in the text makes you think so?

Literary Elements

C1

Using a Venn diagram, compare and contrast the characters Arachne and Athena.

ARACHNE AND ATHENA

Short Stories   **27**

Rumpel-Stilts-Ken

By Jacob Grimm and Wilhelm Grimm

By the side of a wood, in a country a long way off, ran a fine stream of water; and upon the stream there stood a mill. The miller's house was close by, and the miller, you must know, had a very beautiful daughter. She was, moreover, very shrewd and clever; and the miller was so proud of her, that he one day told the king of the land, who used to come and hunt in the wood, that his daughter could spin gold out of straw. Now this king was very fond of money; and when he heard the miller's boast his greediness was raised, and he sent for the girl to be brought before him. Then he led her to a chamber in his palace where there was a great heap of straw, and gave her a spinning-wheel, and said, "All this must be spun into gold before morning, as you love your life." It was in vain that the poor maiden said that it was only a silly boast of her father, for that she could do no such thing as spin straw into gold: the chamber door was locked, and she was left alone.

She sat down in one corner of the room, and began to bewail her hard fate; when on a sudden the door opened, and a droll-looking little man hobbled in, and said, "Good morrow to you, my good lass; what are you weeping for?" "Alas!" said she, "I must spin this straw into gold, and I know not how." "What will you give me," said the hob-goblin, "to do it for you?" "My necklace," replied the maiden. He took her at her word, and sat himself down to the wheel, and whistled and sang—

> "Round about, round about,
> Lo and Behold!
> Reef away, reef away,
> Straw into gold!"

And round about the wheel went merrily; the work was quickly done, and the straw was all spun into gold.

When the king came and saw this, he was greatly astonished and pleased; but his heart grew still more greedy of gain, and he shut up the poor miller's daughter again with a fresh task. Then she knew not what to

Name: _____   Date: _____

do, and sat down once more to weep; but the dwarf soon opened the door, and said, "What will you give me to do your task?" "The ring on my finger," said she. So her little friend took the ring, and began to work at the wheel again, and whistled and sang—

> "Round about, round about,
> Lo and Behold!
> Reef away, reef away,
> Straw into gold!"

till, long before morning, all was done again.

The king was greatly delighted to see all this glittering treasure; but still he had not enough: so he took the miller's daughter to a yet larger heap, and said, "All this must be spun to-night; and if it is, you shall be my queen." As soon as she was alone the dwarf came in, and said, "What will you give me to spin gold for you this third time?" "I have nothing left," said she. "Then say you will give me," said the little man, "the first little child that you may have when you are queen." "That may never be," thought the miller's daughter: and as she knew no other way to get her task done, she said she would do what he asked. Round went the wheel again to the old song, and the manikin once more spun the heap into gold. The king came in the morning, and, finding all he wanted, was forced to keep his word; so he married the miller's daughter, and she really became queen.

At the birth of her first little child she was very glad, and forgot the dwarf, and what she had said. But one day he came into her room, where she was sitting playing with her baby, and put her in mind of it. Then she grieved sorely at her misfortune, and said she would give him all the wealth of the kingdom if he would let her off, but in vain; till at last her tears softened him, and he said, "I will give you three days' grace, and if during that time you tell me my name, you shall keep your child."

Now the queen lay awake all night, thinking of all the odd names that she had ever heard; and she sent messengers all over the land to find out new ones. The next day the little man came, and she began with Timothy, Ichabod, Benjamin, Jeremiah, and all the names she could remember; but to all and each of them he said, "Madam, that is not my name."

The second day she began with all the comical names she could hear of, Bandy-legs, Hunch-back, Crook-shanks, and so on; but the little gentleman still said to every one of them, "Madam, that is not my name." The third day one of the messengers came back, and said, "I travelled two days without

Short Stories   29

hearing of any other names; but yesterday, as I was climbing a high hill, among the trees of the forest where the fox and the hare bid each other good night, I saw a little hut; and before the hut burnt a fire; and round about the fire a funny little dwarf was dancing upon one leg, and singing,—

"'Merrily the feast I'll make,
To-day I'll brew, to-morrow bake;
Merrily I'll dance and sing,
For next day will a stranger bring.
Little does my lady dream
Rumpel-stilts-ken is my name!'"

When the queen heard this she jumped for joy, and as soon as her little friend came she sat down upon her throne, and called all her court round to enjoy the fun; and the nurse stood by her side with the baby in her arms, as if it was quite ready to be given up. Then the little man began to chuckle at the thoughts of having the poor child, to take home with him to his hut in the woods; and he cried out, "Now, lady, what is my name?" "Is it John?" asked she. "No, madam!" "Is it Tom?" "No, madam!" "Is it Jemmy?" "It is not." "Can your name be Rumpel-stilts-ken?" said the lady slyly. "Some witch told you that!—some witch told you that!" cried the little man, and dashed his right foot in a rage so deep into the floor, that he was forced to lay hold of it with both hands to pull it out.

Then he made the best of his way off, while the nurse laughed and the baby crowed; and all the court jeered at him for having had so much trouble for nothing, and said, "We wish you a very good morning, and a merry feast, Mr. Rumpel-stilts-ken!"

Name: _____ Date: _____

Consequences and Implications

A3

How might the story have been different if the following had happened:
- The hobgoblin (dwarf) had not spun the straw into gold for the miller's daughter?
- The miller's daughter had not promised her firstborn child to the hobgoblin (dwarf) for spinning the straw into gold?
- The messenger had not heard the hobgoblin (dwarf) singing his name?

Cause and Effect

A2

Why do you think the hobgoblin (dwarf) "dashed his foot in a rage" when the queen said his name?

Sequencing

A1

List the six most important events of the story in order.

Name: _____ Date: _____

Main Idea, Theme, or Concept

C3

Theme: What is one of the themes explored in the story? What evidence do you have to support your answer?

Inference

C2

If given the opportunity, do you think the hobgoblin (dwarf) would have done anything differently? What evidence supports your position?

Literary Elements

C1

What do you know about the miller's daughter from this story? Support your answer with evidence from the text.

RUMPEL-STILTS-KEN

The Three Painters
By Anne Cao

The kingdom of Norman thrived with color and talent. One could not walk around the village without seeing paintings and tapestries of every color. Around every corner, there were dancers and singers performing to the lively music of talented instrumentalists. Norman was so colorful that it was rumored that every color in the world could be found there. All the trees around the village bore leaves as white as the snow, and the sea shone as blue as the beautiful sky above. The world's best and most renowned artists were born and raised there. Even the ruler, King Leopold, could be found painting works as purple as the lilacs that grew in the kingdom. Nevertheless, underneath all the beauty, Norman had its shadows. Poverty and hunger still ate away at the kingdom.

Many centuries ago, in a nearby village, three brothers lost their parents and their home in a tragic fire. To find a new home, they made their way to Norman. They quickly adapted to the bustling environment and soon became three talented painters. They used dyes made from berries and painted the white leaves that grew around Norman. Their paintings depicted the picturesque, scenic views of the kingdom; their paintings were as beautiful as Norman itself.

Although their works of art were magnificent, the three brothers were not known for their works, nor were they rich. They could not find any money or a home to live in. They lived on the streets and scavenged for anything they could find. Food and water were hard to come by and became as rare as diamonds. Living in Norman, the three brothers came to understand the life of poverty. Every time they asked for food, the other villagers would look away in shame. They walked door-to-door asking for any job, but they were rejected. They always got the same answer. The three brothers had become nobodies.

Soon enough, the brothers were about to die, and they even looked like corpses. They had not eaten anything in days. For another three days and three nights, the three brothers stumbled around the village begging for anything. They huddled together, trying to capture any warmth or strength left in them. Their clothes were like rags, and their blankets were full of lice. They became weaker and weaker until they became as feeble as sick old men. They became as tired as if they had worked nonstop for several days; they were so depressed that they felt like giving up.

On the third day, King Leopold the Third happened to stroll around the village in disguise to examine his kingdom up close. He looked up from his robe, absorbing all the color and beauty of his kingdom. He smiled, seeing how beautiful and successful it was. He did not see his kingdom in darkness, nor did he see the poverty that haunted the village. In his eyes, Norman was perfect the way it was.

On the third night, King Leopold was about to leave the village to make his way to his palace when he saw three skinny hunched figures by the gates. The king's face scrunched in confusion. What had happened to these children? He stepped closer.

By this time, the oldest brother had noticed a strange man looking at them. He considered running away, but there was no strength left in him. Instead, he squinted toward the man, trying to determine who this man was. He had never seen him in the village during his begging rounds. The stranger must not have been from around there.

King Leopold approached the brothers carefully. They looked fragile, like orphans without a home. When he came to a reasonable distance, the king tried to talk to them.

"Where are you parents?"

The oldest brother looked up at the king in confusion. What did he want from them? "Dead," he replied sadly.

"Have you had any food, or perhaps a home?"

"My brothers and I haven't seen food in weeks, nor have we found a home."

The king, utterly shocked, bent down to the brothers' level. He reached for his bag for the leftovers from his lunch. The oldest brother's face lit up in realization. He shook his brothers awake. Weak from starvation, the other brothers struggled to sit up, but when they saw the food, they bolted straight up. The oldest brother hesitated, unsure whether to take the stranger's food. The king shrugged and urged them to take the food. At this gesture, the three brothers snatched the food and began to gobble it down. It was enough to last the brothers for days! The king looked down at this sight and smiled; for once, he had brought light to the darkness. As for the brothers, they regained their hope as well as their strength.

After the stranger revealed himself to be King Leopold, the three brothers wanted to repay him somehow. They bargained with the king for many days. They tried to become servants at the palace. They tried sneaking into the palace to see the king. They even disguised themselves as the royal guards to get the chance to talk with the king.

When the king finally obliged to talk, they were overjoyed. After hours of urging, King Leopold finally acceded to a deal. To repay the king, the three brothers were to paint all of the white leaves that grew around Norman the exact same hue and color.

Because King Leopold was generous, the three brothers were granted luxurious guest rooms within the palace. They received filling, extravagant meals every day. They had servants who dressed them. Best of all, they were dubbed as the Royal Painters of Norman.

After a couple of days of relaxation, the three brothers set off to work. They each made their own color of paint. The oldest brother made a paint as green as the moss that grew on the rocks. The second brother made a paint as orange as the sunset. The youngest brother made a paint as brown as chocolate.

The three brothers soon discovered that they could not agree on the same color to paint the snow-white leaves. The oldest brother wanted the leaves to be green. The second brother wanted the leaves to be orange. The youngest brother wanted the leaves to be brown.

The oldest brother set off to solve the problem his way. On the first night, he cleverly snuck out of the guest rooms, past the guards, and out into the village. He painted every single leaf on every single tree moss green. When he was finished, he snuck back in.

On the second morning, the other brothers were furious with the oldest brother. How could he possibly paint the leaves without their consent? The second brother, seeking revenge, decided to solve the problem his way. Hence, on the second night, the second brother tiptoed out of the palace and into the dark alleys of the village. There, he painted gingerly over every single green leaf with sunset orange.

On the third morning, the other brothers were once again furious. Instead of working together to solve the problem that they had created, the second brother solved the problem himself. The third brother, wanting to solve the problem once and for all, decided to solve the problem his way. Therefore, on the third night, the youngest brother snuck out of the castle and into the villager's booths. There, he sloppily painted over every single orange leaf with chocolate brown. Instead of stopping there, he tore every single leaf off and scattered them all around the village.

The next morning, King Leopold was very disappointed with the brothers' work. The trees used to bear the snow-white leaves year round, but since the youngest brother had torn them all out, the leaves would only stay

Name: _____   Date: _____

on the tree for three-quarters of the year. The king did not know how to deal with the three brothers.

King Leopold was struck with a problem. The brothers had tried to repay him by painting the leaves around the kingdom, but instead they had damaged the kingdom's property. The king, being the civilized man he was, did not want to execute the three brothers, nor did he want to teach the civilians that it was fine to destroy Norman.

After hours of indecision, the king came up with a pact. He called for the three brothers.

"I have come to a decision," the king said solemnly.

"What is it, your majesty?" the oldest brother asked.

"For your actions against the kingdom, you three shall be stripped of your title. You are no longer allowed in the palace. In addition, I am exiling you three from the kingdom of Norman. You are no longer to return to this kingdom ever again."

The three brothers sputtered in surprise. They weren't even allowed in the kingdom anymore. They hadn't done anything severe. Had they? The oldest brother tried to negotiate with the king, but nothing would change the king's mind.

"You may leave now," the king responded.

The three brothers, now with sad faces, were escorted from the palace. Royal guards accompanied them to the outer gates of Norman. Although the three brothers were filled with melancholy, they walked out of the kingdom, and they never looked back.

Outside of Norman, the world was not as colorful. The landscape was as dark as the night sky without the moon. Once again, the three brothers struggled to survive, revisiting their life of poverty. They could not find a job or a home. They never fit in the neighboring village. They rarely found food; there were not many people that were as generous as King Leopold.

From then on, the trees no longer bore white leaves. Instead, they changed color throughout the year. In the spring and the summer, the leaves bore the oldest brother's moss green hue. In the autumn, the leaves bore the second brother's sunset orange hue. In the winter, the leaves fell from the trees and bore the youngest brother's chocolate brown hue. The dynamic colors of the leaves constantly reminded the three brothers to work together instead of disagreeing. The three brothers learned to put their differences behind them, and they learned that they worked best when they worked together as one mind.

Note. Originally published in *Creative Kids* magazine, Winter 2014. Reprinted with permission of Prufrock Press.

Name: _____ Date: _____

Generalizations

B3

What generalizations can you make about the
type of person King Leopold is?

Classifications

B2

Using the lists you created in B1, create a Venn diagram of the
characteristics of the three painters and King Leopold.

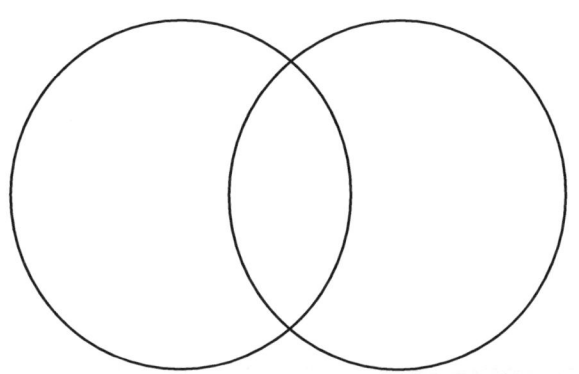

Details

B1

List details about the following characters from the story:
- The three painters
- King Leopold

THE THREE PAINTERS

Short Stories   37

Name: _____ Date: _____

Main Idea, Theme, or Concept

C3

Theme: What are some of the themes explored in the story? What evidence do you have to support your answer?

Inference

C2

If given the opportunity, do you think the three painters would live their lives differently? What evidence supports your position?

Literary Elements

C1

What do you know about King Leopold from this story? Support your answer with evidence from the text.

THE THREE PAINTERS

Name: _____ Date: _____

The Fox and the Cat
Originally told by Aesop

A fox was boasting to a cat about his clever devices for escaping his enemies: "I have a whole bag of tricks," he said, "which contains a hundred ways of escaping my enemies."

"I have only one," said the cat, "but I can generally manage with that." Just at that moment, they heard the cry of a pack of hounds coming towards them, and the cat immediately scampered up a tree and hid herself in the boughs. "This is my plan," said the cat. "What are you going to do?" The fox thought first of one way, then another, and while he was debating the hounds came nearer and nearer. At last, the fox in his confusion was caught up by the hounds and soon killed by the huntsmen.

Name: _____ Date: _____

THE FOX AND THE CAT

Generalizations

B3

Think about the categories you created for the fox's potential means of escape. Now, think about the cat's method of escape. What generalizations can you make about the fox's predicament?

Classifications

B2

Look at the list you created in Question B1. Put the methods of escape that the fox might use into categories.

Details

B1

The fox in the fable boasted about his "whole bag of tricks" for escaping enemies. List at least 25 methods the fox might use to escape.

40 Jacob's Ladder Reading Comprehension Program: GRADE 4

Name: _____ Date: _____

Main Idea, Theme, or Concept

C3

Concept: A sample concept map is started for you about how the story illustrates the concept of "success." Complete the concept map here and then create a concept map of your own on "change," "right and wrong," or another idea.

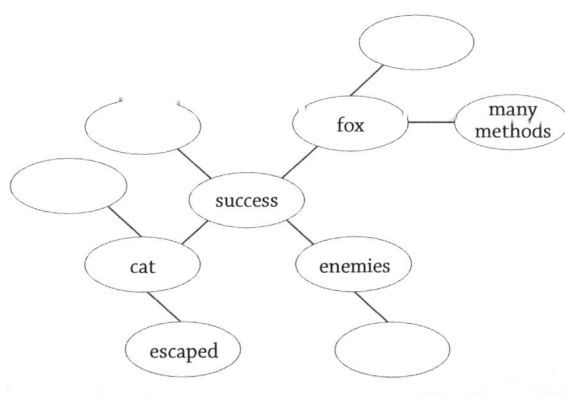

- success
  - fox — many methods
  - (blank)
  - cat — escaped
  - enemies — (blank)

Inference

C2

What inferences can you make about the kind of people the fox and the cat would be if they were human? What evidence from the text supports your inferences?

Literary Elements

C1

Using a Venn diagram, compare and contrast the fox and the cat.

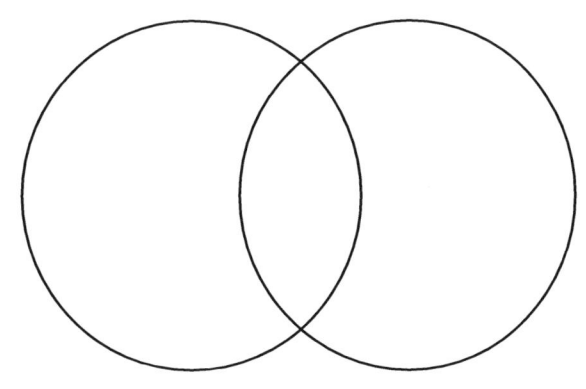

THE FOX AND THE CAT

Short Stories 41

The Lost Wig
Originally told by Aesop

A funny old lion, who had the misfortune to lose his mane, was wearing a wig as he was taking a stroll on a very windy day.

Looking up, he spied one of the charming Tiger sisters across the street, and, wishing to make an impression, smiled blandly and made a beautiful low bow. At that moment a very smart gust of wind came up, and the consequence was that his wig flew off and left him there, feeling foolish and looking worse, with his bald head glistening like a billiard ball. Though somewhat embarrassed at first, he smiled at the Lady and said: "Is it a wonder that another fellow's hair shouldn't keep on my head, when my own wouldn't stay there?"

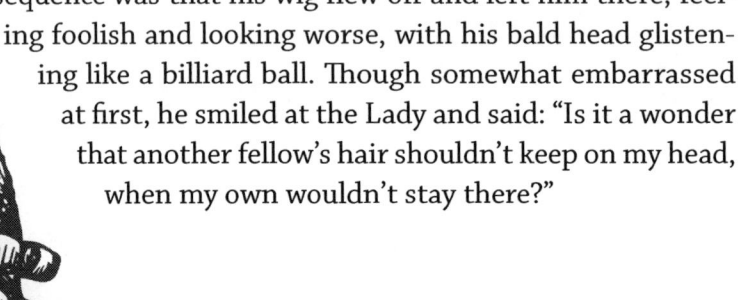

Name: _____ Date: _____

Consequences and Implications

A3

What do you think might happen next in the fable? Defend your ideas.

Cause and Effect

A2

What caused the lion to bow? What was the effect of his actions?

Sequencing

A1

List five events that occur in the fable in order.

THE LOST WIG

Name: _____ Date: _____

Main Idea, Theme, or Concept

C3

Theme: Write a moral for this fable and defend your choice.

Inference

C2

What do you think the lion expected would happen when he bowed? What evidence supports your answer?

Literary Elements

C1

Draw a picture or write a description of the lion. What are his most important characteristics? Why?

THE LOST WIG

Name: _____ Date: _____

Finding the Writer Inside
By Dina Millerman

Maloura was a beautiful mermaid with a face as round as the moon, skin just as pale, and hair that shone like the stars.

No, no. This wouldn't work. I crumpled up the paper. It was so stupid. I mean, writing about mermaids in sixth grade? That's not appropriate. I sighed. I couldn't do creative writing to save my life. How was I supposed to succeed in the current English unit? And, an even better question, why couldn't I write when everyone else could?

The next day at school, Ms. Abbott, my English teacher, gave the worst assignment ever. We had the whole period to write an original short story in our writer's notebooks. I was going to fail.

I sat at my desk for 45 minutes, and still, the paper was blank. I drew a smiley face. Erased it. I wrote "Once Upon a Time . . . ." Erased it.

I looked around at all the kids scribbling away excitedly in their notebooks. How was everyone else so good at this? How did everyone think it was so fun?

I tried to write a few prompts.
The ogre almost killed me.
The putrid smell of coffee filled the air.
I was sitting in school when something strange happened.
Faces at orphanages are young and round, like the sun, only without the smile or the light.

No. I erased everything. All those ideas were flat, featureless, and boring. I looked at the clock. Five minutes left and all my paper had was smudges and pencil marks.

"Everyone, time's up!" Ms. Abbott called out. "Hand your notebooks to me on your way out."

Oh, great! The guilt crashed down around me. My English grade was going to go lower than it already was. I walked out, handing the notebook to Ms. Abbott, and tried not to grab it out of her hands. This was horrible!

I walked to lunch, and sat down next to my best friend Cherylin at our usual table.

"Reed, what did you write for your creative writing assignment?" she asked. "I had the *best* story. So, there's this girl named Sienna. She is the absolute *best* person in her school at basketball, but her mom wants her to focus

Short Stories   45

on her grades more because they're plummeting down. Then, one day, Sienna wakes up and she is suddenly horrible at basketball, but is getting all A's and all the correct answers at school. Her friend, who is the complete opposite of her is now great at basketball, and getting horrible grades. They finally realize they have switched personalities. But how do they switch back? So they do all this research and end up doing this crazy, spooky, old ritual at midnight under the full moon with a million lit candles and are switched back. Isn't it awesome?" Cherylin babbled.

"Mmmm-hmmmm," I mumbled, chewing my sandwich. I didn't mention that I thought the whole idea and plot was kind of lame, but it was a lot better than anything (or nothing) I came up with.

"What did you write, Reed?" Cherylin asked. "Um, I kind of didn't write anything," I mumbled. "What? I didn't catch that."

"I didn't write anything," I mumbled again.

"WHAT? Reed, speak up. I can't hear you!" Cherylin almost screamed.

"I didn't write anything, OK! You know how horrible I am at creative writing. I couldn't come up with any good ideas! Now stop bugging me about it!"

"Sheesh, I was just asking." A glum mood settled over like a wet blanket as we bit into our sandwiches.

The next day, I was dreading English. When fifth period came, I dragged my heavy feet to classroom 214 and plopped into my seat.

"Today," Ms. Abbott announced, "we are doing another creative writing task. You may start a new one, or continue the one you wrote yesterday. You may start writing now."

A couple seconds later, she called out, "Reed, come see me at my desk." I walked up to her. She was holding my notebook. Uh-oh.

Ms. Abbott opened the notebook to yesterday's blank page and glared at me.

"This, Reed, is not acceptable for 45 minutes of work. We are doing the same thing again today, and I expect you to have *something* written down," Ms. Abbot sternly lectured me. Her voice changed to a kind tone and her eyes softened. "At least a couple sentences, OK?"

"I'll try," I said, looking at the ground.

"And Reed, show me your notebook at the end of class. I want to see how you do."

Name: _____ Date: _____

For a million years, I just sat there. Same thing as yesterday. All over again. It didn't help that Ms. Abbott was peering at me through her pointy glasses. Finally, with 5 minutes of the period left, that horrible little sentence came back to me again. The one about the mermaid. The one that I absolutely despised. But, at least it was something, and Ms. Abbott had been very clear when she said she wanted something, anything, at least. So I wrote it down. Slowly, carefully. Soon, the same words I had written before appeared on my paper.

Maloura was a beautiful mermaid with a face as round as the moon, skin just as pale, and hair that shone like the stars.

I still hated it, don't get me wrong, but Ms. Abbott, well, she really wanted something. And she was a big fan of figurative language. So I wrote it down and gave it a rest. I had written the very most that could come to my mind. I couldn't come up with any continuation. The bell rang.

"Everyone, you may now go to lunch. Reed, please come see me with your notebook." I walked up to Ms. Abbott, notebook in hand, semi-proud of the one measly sentence.

As she read the sentence, I watched her face for a sign, but nothing gave away what she was thinking.

"Reed, this is wonderful! It's only one sentence, and you should've written more, but I love the figurative language and the idea of mermaids. Great start! You have got a writer inside you; you just have to find it. Have this story finished by Monday."

I went to lunch, brimming with ideas.

Note. Originally published in *Creative Kids* magazine, Fall 2016. Reprinted with permission of Prufrock Press.

Name: _____ Date: _____

Main Idea, Theme, or Concept

C3

Theme: Why did the author share this story with the world? What ideas does she want to share?

Inference

C2

The narrator seems to have problems getting started with her writing. What evidence supports this? What inferences can you make about the narrator based on the story?

Literary Elements

C1

List examples of how the author used dialogue to enhance her story.

FINDING THE WRITER INSIDE

Name: _____ Date: _____

Creative Synthesis

D3

This story portrays an example of how someone might feel when he or she is uneasy about completing a certain task. Use the story as a model to create your own story about your uneasiness in trying to complete a task.

Summarizing

D2

Summarize the main idea of the selection in five sentences or fewer.

Paraphrasing

D1

Rewrite the following paragraph in your own words:

No, no. This wouldn't work. I crumpled up the paper. It was so stupid. I mean, writing about mermaids in sixth grade? That's not appropriate. I sighed. I couldn't do creative writing to save my life. How was I supposed to succeed in the current English unit? And, an even better question, why couldn't I write when everyone else could?

FINDING THE WRITER INSIDE

Short Stories   49

The Myth of Athena

One day, Metis, wife of Zeus, came to her husband with joyous news: She was going to have a baby. At first, Zeus was ecstatic. He wanted a son or a daughter to whom he could show his power over Greece. However, his enthusiasm for his new son or daughter was short-lived. One of Zeus's trusted advisors told him he should be wary of a child. His advisor asked Zeus, "What if you have a son and your son overthrows you as you overthrew your father?" Zeus became worried. He decided he could not allow Metis to have her child, so he swallowed her whole.

After a while, Zeus developed a terrible headache. He was unable to determine the cause of his pain, and his trusted advisor had no answers. The pain continued to increase until one morning Zeus's skull split open! From this chasm, a daughter, Athena emerged. Because Zeus had swallowed Metis whole, he also had absorbed all of her wisdom. The combined wisdom of Zeus and Metis was passed on to Athena, who became the goddess of wisdom.

Athena led a very exciting life. In addition to being the goddess of wisdom, Athena also became known as the goddess of war. She helped many of the heroes of the Trojan War achieve victory through her tactical knowledge and the strategies of war.

Athena was revered by the Greeks for her wisdom and is credited with many important inventions, such as the wagon, the flute, shoemaking, shipbuilding, and the plough. Through the years, Greeks and their successors have said Athena provided mankind with all of the necessary knowledge to build the foundation of a civilization.

Name: _____   Date: _____

Consequences and Implications

A3 Choose three of the inventions that are credited to Athena. How would life be different if these inventions did not exist? Explain your answer.

Cause and Effect

A2 Why did Athena have so much wisdom? Support your answer with evidence from the text.

Sequencing

A1 List the five most important events of the myth in order.

THE MYTH OF ATHENA

Short Stories 51

Name: _____ Date: _____

Creative Synthesis

D3

Create your own story that explains how wisdom can win wars.

Summarizing

D2

Summarize how being the goddess of wisdom would be helpful to Athena in her role as goddess of war.

Paraphrasing

D1

In your own words, explain why Athena was revered by the Greeks.

THE MYTH OF ATHENA

The Myth of Heracles (Hercules)

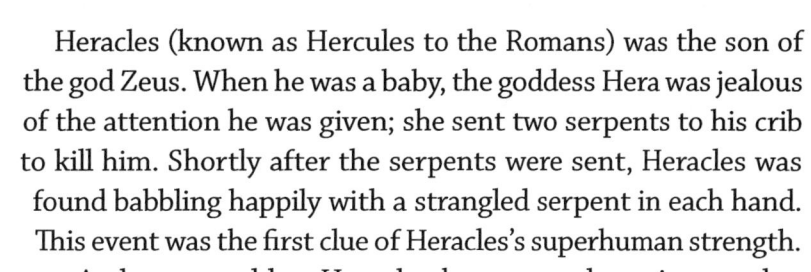

Heracles (known as Hercules to the Romans) was the son of the god Zeus. When he was a baby, the goddess Hera was jealous of the attention he was given; she sent two serpents to his crib to kill him. Shortly after the serpents were sent, Heracles was found babbling happily with a strangled serpent in each hand. This event was the first clue of Heracles's superhuman strength.

As he grew older, Heracles became a champion marksman and wrestler. Unfortunately, he was driven mad by Hera and in a frenzy of anger killed his own children. To atone for this terrible deed, Heracles was charged with completing 12 tasks, or labors, for his cousin, King Eurystheus. The 12 labors were thought to be impossible; everyone believed Heracles would die trying to accomplish them.

The first labor Heracles was given was to slay the Nemean lion. This was no ordinary lion. Arrows or spears could not penetrate its skin. Heracles defeated the lion by blocking the entrance to his den and killing it with his bare hands. When Heracles returned carrying the defeated Nemean lion, everyone, including Eurystheus, was in awe of his strength.

One of the more exciting tasks for Heracles was to slay the much-feared Hydra. No one is entirely sure how many heads the Hydra had; some believe it was eight or nine, while others claim the Hydra had 10,000 heads! There was agreement, though, about the Hydra's ability to regrow two heads for every one that was cut off. As if many heads were not frightening enough, the Hydra's breath was lethal to mere mortals. Fortunately for Heracles, he was not a mere mortal. With the help of his nephew, Iolaus (who just happened to be waiting in the chariot), Heracles cut off each of the Hydra's heads while Iolaus seared the wound, making it impossible for another head to grow.

Heracles's final task was to bring back Cerberus from the Underworld, the land of the dead. His first obstacle was getting across the River Styx, the most famous river of the Underworld where all of the dead souls congregated. Heracles could not pay the bribe to Charon the Boatman, nor was he dead; both of these were prerequisites for entering the Underworld. Heracles had to use his superhuman strength to frighten Charon into taking him across the River Styx. Once in the Underworld, Heracles was confronted with Cerberus and his razor-sharp teeth and venomous snake tail. Luckily, Heracles was wearing the armor he made from the Nemean lion that he had slain during the first labor. The lion's skin was impenetrable to Cerberus's teeth or tail. Heracles eventually succeeded at this labor as well.

Many years later after many more adventures, Heracles died from wearing a tunic tainted by poison, much to the dismay of his beloved wife Deianara.

Name: _____ Date: _____

Consequences and Implications

A3

Why was Heracles's manner of death ironic? Explain.

Cause and Effect

A2

What caused Heracles to be tasked with the 12 labors? What effects did the assignment have on his life?

Sequencing

A1

List the five most important events in the myth in order.

THE MYTH OF HERACLES (HERCULES)

Name: _____ Date: _____

THE MYTH OF HERACLES (HERCULES)

Creative Synthesis

D3

Create a myth that has a crime and punishment theme like the Heracles myth.

Summarizing

D2

In three sentences or fewer, summarize the main idea of the myth.

Paraphrasing

D1

In your own words, rewrite one of the labors described in the myth.

Short Stories 55

Name: _____ Date: _____

Theseus and the Minotaur

Theseus and his father, King Aegeus, were very close. One day, while they were enjoying the pleasant scenery in the palace garden, a woman came to visit King Aegeus. She begged the king not to send her son to Crete. Not understanding why the woman was asking his father for her son's salvation, Theseus asked the king why the boy would have to go to Crete. King Aegeus explained to his son that every year King Minos, ruler of Crete, demanded seven boys and seven girls be sent to him from Athens for the Minotaur. Theseus asked what King Minos did with the young people sent to him. King Aegeus responded that, unfortunately, he did not know. All of the boys and girls who had been sent to Crete had never been heard from again.

Theseus took a few moments to think about what his father had said. Then, he placed his hands on the woman's shoulders and told her not to worry. Her son would not be going to Crete because he, Theseus, would go in his place. King Aegeus became distraught. "You cannot go!" he exclaimed to Theseus. "You must become king one day." Theseus told his father that he would grow up to be a much better king if he were able to save Athens from King Minos's demands. "I will go to Crete and slay the Minotaur!" cried Theseus.

The next morning, Theseus was preparing for his voyage. His father came to him to explain why his ship had a black sail. If Theseus was successful in slaying the Minotaur, he was to change the sail to white. Every day, King Aegeus would stand on the cliff overlooking the sea, watching for his son's ship to return. If the sail was white, he would know Theseus had been successful; if the sail was black, he would know Theseus had been slaughtered.

For many days the ship sailed until it finally arrived at Crete. All the people of Crete had gathered to see Theseus's arrival. In the crowd was King Minos's daughter, Ariadne. When she saw Theseus, she immediately fell in love with him. She knew of her father's plans to feed Theseus to the Minotaur; she also knew she could not let Theseus be killed.

Late that night, Ariadne came to Theseus's cell. She told him to follow her very quietly. Ariadne took Theseus to the labyrinth where the

Minotaur lived. "Always turn to the right—that is the secret of the labyrinth," said Ariadne. Then, she handed him a sword and a spool of golden thread to mark his path as he went farther and farther into the maze. Theseus remembered Ariadne's words and always turned to the right. He could hear the Minotaur's roaring growing louder and louder. Suddenly, the Minotaur was before him! Theseus attacked, plunging the sword deep into the heart of the ferocious beast. Once he was sure the Minotaur no longer lived, Theseus followed the golden thread out of the labyrinth and into the waiting arms of his beloved Ariadne.

Theseus and Ariadne knew King Minos would be furious when he discovered what had happened. They rapidly ran to Theseus's ship and began the journey back to Athens. King Minos's men quickly began their pursuit and for many hours Theseus was uncertain of their escape from the ships of Crete. Finally, they appeared to have outrun King Minos's men. Ariadne, Theseus, and the crew of the ship decided to spend the night on the island of Naxos. In the morning, however, one of the shipmen saw the ships from Crete approaching. They were once again in danger of being captured. Everyone rushed to the ship and quickly set sail. After outrunning King Minos's men again, Theseus realized that Ariadne had been left on the island of Naxos. He desperately wanted to go back for her, but his men convinced him they would all be captured and killed if they turned back. Saddened, Theseus told his shipmates to continue sailing toward Athens.

In all of the excitement, Theseus had forgotten to change the sail from black to white. King Aegeus, who had kept his word and watched for his son everyday from the cliff overlooking the sea, saw the black sail and began to despair. Deciding he did not want to continue living if his son had been killed by the Minotaur, King Aegeus flung himself off the cliff and into the sea (which, to this day, is known as the Aegean sea).

Name: _____ Date: _____

Generalizations

B3

What generalizations about bravery can you write using the list and categories you created? How do the generalizations you created apply to this story?

Classifications

B2

Using the list you generated in question B1, create categories of the different ways someone can be brave. Use all of the items from your list.

Details

B1

Theseus acted bravely in this myth by facing the Minotaur. List at least 25 different ways a person can be brave.

THESEUS AND THE MINOTAUR

Name: _____ Date: _____

Creative Synthesis

D3

In ancient times, the same myth was often told from multiple points of view. Retell the myth of "Theseus and the Minotaur" from another character's point of view (e.g., Ariadne, King Minos, King Aegeus).

Summarizing

D2

In five sentences or fewer, summarize the main ideas of this myth.

Paraphrasing

D1

In your own words, retell what happened to Theseus while he was on the island of Crete.

THESEUS AND THE MINOTAUR

Short Stories 59

Chapter 2

Poetry

Chapter 2 includes the selected readings and accompanying question sets for each poetry selection. Each reading is followed by two sets of questions; each set is aligned to one of the four ladder skills.

For *Jacob's Ladder, Grade 4*, the skills covered by each selection are as follows:

Poetry	Ladder Skills
I Am Autumn	C, C
13 Ways of Looking at a Rose	B, C
Sweet Summer	B, C
My Shadow	B, C
After the Winter	B, C
Travel	B, C
Saving Words	A, C
Dubstep	B, C
Approach of Winter	B, C

I Am Autumn
By Victoria Krylova

I creep behind the sunny meadows
Whirling my flaming gown
I spin the laces of mist and dew
Of frost and crystal ice
I shake hands with the poppies
They wilt at the sight of my glare
I sentence death to the fields of green
Spilling red and yellow on the trees
I dip my finger in the snoozing lakes
Freezing their lazy countenance
I poke the bears into their dens
And call out the snow owls
I splatter the scent of cold and rain
And shower sleet from the clouds
I twirl my hair and hear the wolves
Howl their starving cry
I gaze at the span of winnowing wind
Who is seeking me?
Who has seen me?
Nobody will stop me
For I will continue to weave
The blanket of frigid death

Note. Originally published in *Creative Kids* magazine, Fall 2015. Reprinted with permission of Prufrock Press.

Name: _____ Date: _____

Main Idea, Theme, or Concept

C3

Theme: Pretend you are collecting poems that are similar to this one to put in a book of poetry. Create a title for the book of poems and create titles for at least four more poems that would belong in a group with this poem. Explain why you chose the titles.

Inference

C2

Infer means "to draw a conclusion based on evidence." From the poem, what can you infer about the author's feelings about autumn? What is the evidence to support your inferences?

Literary Elements

C1

Personification is when an author gives human qualities to something that is not human. What are some examples of personification in this poem?

I AM AUTUMN

Name: _____ Date: _____

Main Idea, Theme, or Concept

C3

Theme/Concept: Using the poem as a model and selecting a season other than autumn, write your own poem called "I Am _____ (name of a season)" that begins: "I creep behind the . . . " Fill in the blank with the name of an animal, person, or other being. Then continue to create a 12-line poem.

Inference

C2

What can you infer about how autumn treats animals and plants? How do you know this?

Literary Elements

C1

Imagery is the use of words or phrases that appeal to any sense or any combination of senses. You can close your eyes and see the image behind the words of the poet. What images do you see from the poem?

I AM AUTUMN

13 Ways of Looking at a Rose
By Sihyun Na

I. Among the ten placid bushes
were the flirtatious roses
warning not to come close.

II. Like Matryoshka Dolls
you can never tell
which is the best.

III. Left alone getting picked off
one by one
falling to the lowest surface possible
the mood and its expression
change simultaneously.
And there stand
deplorable petals of a rose.

IV. Carefully chosen and
wrapped in the finest way possible,
it is held in a man's hand
to make a perfect moment.

V. I do not know which to prefer,
the excitement of a rosebud
or the beauty of one bloomed.

VI. Cut from the steady branches,
the roses are gathered in a
delicate vase to brighten the room.

VII. Astonished by the color
of the rose petal,
the man reached out
only to get his own rose
on his ring finger
as he cried out in pain.

VIII. As the weather roared
scaring every little kid around,
the rose stood fighting
against the wind
showing a struggle
only when lightning struck.

IX. On the porcelain cup
there was an antique rose

        drawn out carefully
        helping the bitter coffee
        look sweeter.

X.   Inside the frame sat a woman
        calmly drinking wine
        looking out to the deep lake
        surrounded by nothing
        but roses for company.

XI.   As the time of sunset changes,
        the roses stand in a line
        waiting for a chance
        to see the world.

XII. Plastics imitating roses
        tied together to make a circle
        big enough to hang on top of a head.

XIII. As I look down on my teacup
        I see flowers floating
        on top of the warm water,
        I see the roses.

Note. Originally published in *Creative Kids* magazine, Summer 2014. Reprinted with permission of Prufrock Press.

Name: _____ Date: _____

Generalizations

B3 Using the titles you created for your groups in B2, write at least three generalizations you can make about a rose. Use evidence from the poem.

Classifications

B2 Review your list of characteristics. Divide them into groups and create a title for each group of characteristics.

Details

B1 Make a list of characteristics of a rose.

13 WAYS OF LOOKING AT A ROSE

Poetry 67

Name: _____ Date: _____

Main Idea, Theme, or Concept

C3

Main Idea: Think about how the author described different ways to look at a rose. Using "13 Ways of Looking at a Rose" as a model, write a new poem about multiple ways of looking at something else. The poem should be at least 16 lines long.

Inference

C2

What feelings do you think the author has about the rose? Why? Use phrases from the poem as evidence to support your inference.

Literary Elements

C1

Personification is when an author gives human characteristics to nonhuman objects. Give examples of personification from the poem.

13 WAYS OF LOOKING AT A ROSE

Sweet Summer
By Morgan Trail

Reaching in, brambles and thorns claw my arms;
birds chirp on nearby bushes and bumblebees hum softly.
Plucking with sticky red and purple stained hands,
softly plunking into my almost full bucket.
The sweet and sour sensation with hairs tickling my tongue.
The perfect one, just out of reach,
leaning, stretching out my arm,
I feel the bumpy, squishy fruit on my fingertips.
Just then, it drops out of sight in the thick brambles.
There goes my perfect blackberry.

Note. Originally published in *Creative Kids* magazine, Summer 2015. Reprinted with permission of Prufrock Press.

Name: _____ Date: _____

Generalizations

B3

What can you generalize about the use of descriptive words in a poem or story? How would stories or poems change if authors used too many or too few descriptive words?

Classifications

B2

Sort the descriptive words and phrases from B1 into categories. Give each category a title.

Details

B1

List the characteristics of a blackberry using the words and phrases in the poem. Look up any words that are unfamiliar to you.

SWEET SUMMER

Name: _____ Date: _____

Main Idea, Theme, or Concept

C3

Main Idea: You are going to write a poem. Select an object in your classroom. That will be the title of the poem. Brainstorm words and phrases you can use to describe that object, including "people" attributes (personification). Write your poem using the words and phrases you brainstormed to explain your object. Read your poem to the class, without saying the title of your poem, and ask them to guess your title.

Inference

C2

Write each line of the poem. Next to the line, explain how that line is a clue to describing the title object.

Literary Elements

C1

Personification is when an author gives human characteristics to non-human objects. Give examples of personification from the poem.

SWEET SUMMER

My Shadow

By Robert Louis Stevenson

I have a little shadow that goes in and out with me,
And what can be the use of him is more than I can see.
He is very, very like me from the heels up to the head;
And I see him jump before me, when I jump into my bed.

The funniest thing about him is the way he likes to grow—
Not at all like proper children, which is always very slow;
For he sometimes shoots up taller like an India-rubber ball,
And he sometimes goes so little that there's none of him at all.

He hasn't got a notion of how children ought to play,
And can only make a fool of me in every sort of way.
He stays so close behind me, he's a coward you can see;
I'd think shame to stick to nursie as that shadow sticks to me!

One morning, very early, before the sun was up,
I rose and found the shining dew on every buttercup;
But my lazy little shadow, like an arrant sleepy-head,
Had stayed at home behind me and was fast asleep in bed.

Name: _____ Date: _____

Generalizations

B3

Write one or two generalizations about shadows.

Classifications

B2

Create categories using the words and phrases from Activity B1. Every word and phrase must fit into one and only one category. Create a title for each group.

Details

B1

Make a list of words and phrases that are used to describe the shadow.

MY SHADOW

Poetry 73

Name: _____ Date: _____

Main Idea, Theme, or Concept

C3

Main Idea: Write one or two sentences that explain what idea the author wanted to share with his readers.

Inference

C2

Make a list of characteristics of a shadow noted in the poem. What inferences can you make about the "character" of the shadow from these characteristics?

Literary Elements

C1

Personification is when an author gives human characteristics to nonhuman objects. Robert Louis Stevenson uses personification in this poem. How does the child describe his shadow to reflect personification? Give examples.

MY SHADOW

After the Winter
By Claude McKay

Some day, when trees have shed their leaves
    And against the morning's white
The shivering birds beneath the eaves
    Have sheltered for the night,
We'll turn our faces southward, love,
    Toward the summer isle
Where bamboos spire to shafted grove
    And wide-mouthed orchids smile.
And we will seek the quiet hill
    Where towers the cotton tree,
And leaps the laughing crystal rill,
    And works the droning bee.
And we will build a cottage there
    Beside an open glade,
With black-ribbed blue-bells blowing near,
    And ferns that never fade.

Name: _____ Date: _____

Generalizations

B3

Write one or two generalizations about the time of year that comes after the winter.

Classifications

B2

Create categories using the words and phrases from Activity B1. Every word and phrase must fit into one and only one category. Create a title for each group.

Details

B1

Make a list of words and phrases that are used to describe the time of year that comes after the winter.

AFTER THE WINTER

Name: _____ Date: _____

Main Idea, Theme, or Concept

C3

Main Idea: Write one or two sentences that explain what ideas the author wanted to share with his readers.

Inference

C2

Make a list of characteristics of the time of year that comes after the winter noted in the poem. What inferences can you make about the "character" of the time after winter from these characteristics?

Literary Elements

C1

Personification is when an author gives human characteristics to nonhuman objects. McKay uses personification in this poem. Give some examples.

AFTER THE WINTER

Travel

By Edna St. Vincent Millay

The railroad track is miles away,
    And the day is loud with voices speaking,
Yet there isn't a train goes by all day
    But I hear its whistle shrieking.
All night there isn't a train goes by,
    Though the night is still for sleep and dreaming,
But I see its cinders red on the sky,
    And hear its engine steaming.
My heart is warm with the friends I make,
    And better friends I'll not be knowing;
Yet there isn't a train I wouldn't take,
    No matter where it's going.

Name: _____ Date: _____

Generalizations

B3

Using your list as a guide, make two general statements about the narrator.

Classifications

B2

Using your list of details, are there any inferences you can make to classify this narrator?

Details

B1

What details do we know about the narrator from the poem?

TRAVEL

Poetry

Name: _____ Date: _____

Main Idea, Theme, or Concept

C3

Main Idea: What important idea about travel does this poem tell us?

Inference

C2

Poems often create feelings in the reader. What feelings does this poem create? Give examples of words from the poem that create these feelings. What inferences can you make about how the use of certain words in a poem helps create mood?

Literary Elements

C1

Imagery is the use of words or phrases that appeal to any sense or any combination of senses. You can close your eyes and see the image behind the words of the poet. What images do you see from the poem?

TRAVEL

Saving Words
By John Vernaglia

My teacher says, "Write a poem, so sit and concentrate."
She says, "Stop delaying and trying to procrastinate."
I sit at the computer and try to find my voice,
But nothing comes right to me, because this is not my choice.
I write a lot of words, but nothing seems to rhyme.
Look at what I've written, it's a literary crime!
The period is almost over, and finally it comes to me.
The poem comes pouring out, literary mastery!
I go to show my teacher, but the computer screen is blank.
My heart begins to crumble, my hope for an "A" sank.
Because there went my poem, oh so carefully written,
All because my computer had trouble with transmittin'.
The moral to the story, for all you kids out there
When you write that perfect poem, save first before you share.

Note. Originally published in *Creative Kids* magazine, Winter 2014. Reprinted with permission of Prufrock Press.

Name: _____ Date: _____

Consequences and Implications

A3

In the poem, the author describes the consequences of not saving his work on his computer properly. Think of a situation when something has been problematic for you, because you made a mistake or due to the fault of something else. Write your own poem, using "Saving Words" as a model.

Cause and Effect

A2

Create a fishbone diagram to show the effects of not saving your work on your computer properly. Use evidence from the poem as your guide. A sample diagram has been included for you.

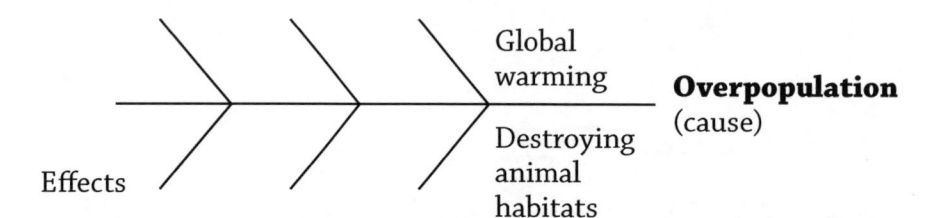

Effects — Global warming — Destroying animal habitats → **Overpopulation** (cause)

Sequencing

A1

List the four most important events of this poem in order.

SAVING WORDS

82   Jacob's Ladder Reading Comprehension Program: GRADE 4

Name: _____ Date: _____

Main Idea, Theme, or Concept

C3

Theme: Using the evidence the author provides and other information you know, write an e-mail from the point of view of the author to his teacher, explaining why he did not submit the poem.

Inference

C2

What does the author mean by "The poem comes pouring out, literary mastery"?

Literary Elements

C1

How does the author use rhyming words in this poem?

SAVING WORDS

Poetry 83

Dubstep

By Victor Frolenko

Found the perfect song
But don't wait too long
Starting off slow
This part's just for show
The beats start building up
Electrical music's stirring up
The rhythm gets louder and louder
Then it reaches its maximum power
Then the music goes completely still
At this time you're pretty much chill
You think there's something wrong
But you hear the name of the song
All of that tension gets cut off
It all feels like a blast-off
DUB-WUB you hear the song go
The intensity of the beat starts to grow
BOOM-BANG the bass goes loud
The strong beats sound like a wicked storm cloud
WUB-WUB the notes stretch out
This's the best song without a doubt
You hear the name repeat once more
By this time you're in the core
The music begins to calm its way down
And you kinda feel an approaching countdown
Tada-tada the next section's starting off
Beginning to feel like a sudden liftoff
DUB-WUB-CRASH you feel your chest pump
The sounds get loud with a steady fast thump
BOOM-BANG-PANG the notes hitting hard
Then there's added sounds like a wild card
WUB-WUB-BUB this rhythm's appealing
You are starting to get a real good feeling
The music slows down and starts to flow
This dubstep makes you feel like a pro
This masterpiece is starting to end
All this time was worthy spent
The last notes are sounding

Name: _____ Date: _____

Your heart is pounding
You are waiting for more
But your ears are sore
But you don't care
These songs are a worthy share.

Note. Originally published in *Creative Kids* magazine, Fall 2016. Reprinted with permission of Prufrock Press.

Name: _____ Date: _____

Generalizations

B3

Write three generalizations about dubstep music.

Classifications

B2

Group these words or phrases into categories and give each group a title.

Details

B1

Make a list of words or phrases that relate to music.

DUBSTEP

86 Jacob's Ladder Reading Comprehension Program: GRADE 4

Name: _____ Date: _____

Main Idea, Theme, or Concept

C3

Main idea: After reading this poem, what ideas do you think the author has about dubstep music?

Inference

C2

Looking at the way each line of the poem ends, describe the feeling you think the author wants the reader to have. What words from the poem support your ideas?

Literary Elements

C1

Onomatopoeia is defined as a word or phrase that imitates the natural sounds of a thing. Make a list of examples of onomatopoeia from the poem.

DUBSTEP

Poetry 87

Approach of Winter
By William Carlos Williams

The half-stripped trees
struck by a wind together,
bending all,
the leaves flutter drily
and refuse to let go
or driven like hail
stream bitterly out to one side
and fall
where the salvias, hard carmine,—
like no leaf that ever was—
edge the bare garden.

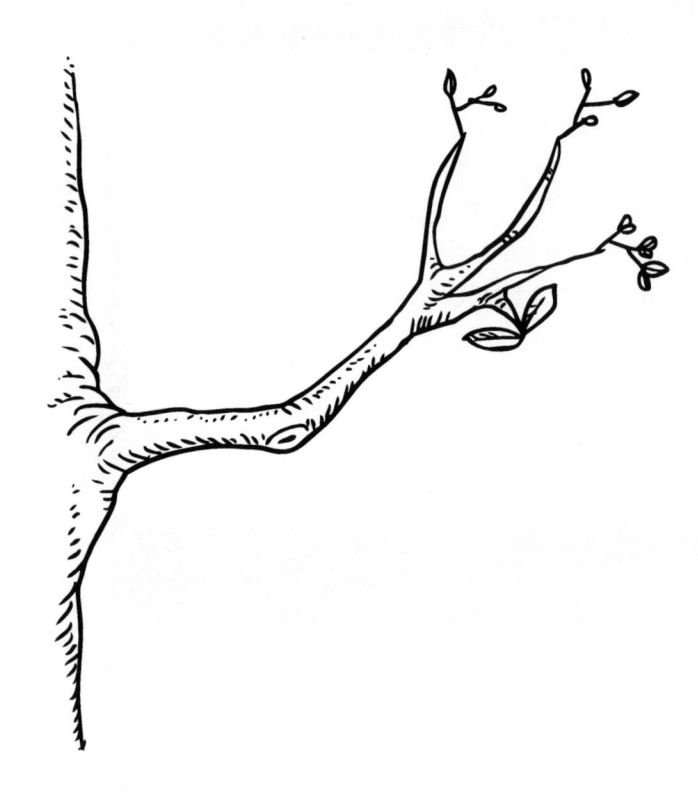

Name: _____ Date: _____

Generalizations

B3

Which generalization best describes the poem?
- Winter is a harsh season.
- Winter changes the landscape.
- Winter approaches by causing big changes.

Why did you select your answer? Use words from the poem to explain your choice in a well-developed paragraph.

Classifications

B2

Create a T-chart. On the left, list phrases the author used to personify the leaves. On the right, list characteristics of leaves that may have caused the author to choose each phrase on the left. Now do the same thing with your list from B1.

Details

B1

Choose an object, like the leaves in the poem, and make a list of human characteristics you would give to your object if you were writing a poem about it.

APPROACH OF WINTER

Poetry **89**

Name: _____ Date: _____

Main Idea, Theme, or Concept

C3

Main Idea: Create a new title that reveals the main idea of the poem.

Inference

C2

Using the words the author chose, what can we infer about his attitude about winter?

Literary Elements

C1

Personification is when an author gives human characteristics to nonhuman objects. Make a list of human characteristics the author gave the leaves.

APPROACH OF WINTER

90 Jacob's Ladder Reading Comprehension Program: GRADE 4

Chapter 3

Nonfiction

Chapter 3 includes the selected readings and accompanying question sets for each nonfiction selection. Each reading is followed by two sets of questions; each set is aligned to one of the four ladder skills.

For *Jacob's Ladder, Grade 4*, the skills covered by each selection are as follows:

Nonfiction	Ladder Skills
The American Revolutionary War	C, D
The Exploration of Space	A, D
Graphic Ice Cream	B, C
The Great Depression	A, B
It's Electric!	B, D
The Metric System vs. the U.S. Customary System	A, C

The American Revolutionary War

In 1765, Americans still considered themselves loyal subjects to the British crown. Great Britain had just finished the Seven Years War with France, during which the Americans helped the British defeat the French on American soil. After the war ended, Great Britain was looking for a way to help pay for the war. Because part of the reason they went to war with France was to protect their colonies in America, the British government decided to pay for the war through taxing Americans. The taxes implemented by the British government were not necessarily high. However, Americans were upset that they were not consulted about the new taxes. The Americans felt it was illegal, or at the very least not fair, to tax them without giving them proper representation within the British parliament. The statement "No taxation without representation" became a well-known phrase during the American Revolutionary War.

The first direct tax against the colonies was the Stamp Act in 1765. The Stamp Act declared that all official documents, newspapers, almanacs, pamphlets, and even playing cards must have official stamps on them. If they did not have stamps, which Americans must buy from Britain, then fines would be charged. Later acts further restricted the activities of Americans. The Currency Act prohibited Americans from printing their own paper money, which hindered trade among the colonies. The Quartering Act mandated that American colonists house British soldiers in their homes, which invaded the colonists' privacy. Colonists began voicing their protests against these taxes and acts. In 1770, the Boston Massacre occurred in Massachusetts. In protest of the Stamp Act and the Tea Act, colonists dumped tea bricks from British ships into Boston Harbor, in what is now known as the Boston Tea Party. During this protest, five Americans were killed.

Because of incidents like this one, as well as philosophical differences between England and the colonies, and America's desire for independence, the American Revolutionary War, also known as the American War of Independence, began in 1775.

In 1776, representatives from each of the 13 colonies met in Philadelphia where they unanimously signed the Declaration of Independence, thereby forming the United States of America. In 1778, the colonists formed an alliance with France. The French helped by sending money, munitions, and troops. These contributions from France helped level the playing field in the war against Britain. However, the Americans were fighting against a monarchy for the right to establish a democracy. Even though France was helping them win their independence, Americans did not view France as a role model.

During the war, only 1/3 of the colonists, known as Patriots, supported war with Britain, 1/3 of colonists, known as Loyalists, remained loyal to Britain, and 1/3 of colonists remained neutral. However, throughout the war, the Patriots maintained control over 80%–90% of the land. The British were able to capture only a few coastal cities, which they gained through their strong Navy presence.

At the Battle at Saratoga in 1777, one of Britain's main armies was captured, the beginning of the end for the British. In 1781, the British army surrendered at the Battle of Yorktown. This surrender led to the signing of the Treaty of Paris for peace in 1783.

Name: _____ Date: _____

Main Idea, Theme, or Concept

C3

Concept: What concept represents why the American Revolutionary War was fought? State your answer in five words or less.

Inference

C2

What inferences can be made about the French becoming allies with the Americans during the American Revolutionary War? Justify your answer.

Literary Elements

C1

Choose to be a Patriot, a Loyalist, or a neutral colonist. Describe your character's point of view regarding the war. Support your answer with details.

THE AMERICAN REVOLUTIONARY WAR

Name: _____ Date: _____

Creative Synthesis

D3

Write a letter to your family about the American Revolutionary War from the point of view of a colonist, a British soldier, or a French soldier. Be sure to include enough details for the recipient of your letter to understand the war from your point of view.

Summarizing

D2

In three sentences or fewer, summarize the cause(s) of the American Revolutionary War.

Paraphrasing

D1

In your own words, rewrite the following statements:
- "No taxation without representation."
- "Even though France was helping them win their independence, Americans did not view France as a role model."

THE AMERICAN REVOLUTIONARY WAR

Nonfiction 95

The Exploration of Space

The exploration of space gives scientists the opportunity to learn about the sun, stars, and planets. Some space exploration involves scientists called *astronauts* traveling into space. Astronauts use spacecraft, such as space shuttles, to travel beyond the Earth's atmosphere into outer space, which begins about 60 miles above sea level. While in outer space, astronauts explore their surroundings with various tools, such as safety tethering systems to keep their spacesuits attached to the spacecraft (and smaller tethers to attach their tools to their spacesuits). Astronauts might also wear a SAFER or Simplified Aid for EVA Rescue (EVA stands for extravehicular activity, another term for spacewalk). A SAFER is like a backpack that uses small jet thrusters to allow an astronaut to move in space. Other space exploration does not require astronauts but instead uses spacecraft with robots or other mechanical devices, such as satellites, to gather information.

In order for spacecraft, manned or unmanned, to travel into outer space, they must first overcome the pull of Earth's gravity. The heavier an object, the more power is required to break the Earth's gravitational pull. As you can imagine, it takes a tremendous amount of power to launch a space shuttle. These large spacecraft require booster rockets full of fuel to launch them. The boosters burn the fuel that gives off gas bursts that push the spacecraft into the air. The spacecraft eventually reaches a height where the Earth's gravitational pull no longer affects it. Once it passes this point, the shuttle only needs to fire rockets to increase its speed or to change directions.

When a spacecraft is ready to return to Earth, it must first slow down. Once it reenters the atmosphere, it slows down considerably and begins falling toward Earth. The spacecraft deploys, or puts into action, parachutes that further slow down its descent. Spacecraft like space shuttles land on runways just like airplanes. Some of the earlier U.S. spacecraft "splashed down" in the ocean where the astronauts were picked up by boats.

On October 4, 1957, the Soviet Union launched Sputnik, a satellite that orbited Earth, and space exploration officially began. Years later, on April 12, 1961, Yuri A. Gagarin, a Soviet cosmonaut, became the first person to travel to space. In December 1968, the U.S. took the first trip to the moon in the spacecraft Apollo 8, orbiting the moon 10 times before returning to Earth. Less than a year later, the American astronaut Neil Armstrong became the first person to walk on the moon on July 20, 1969. As Armstrong placed the American flag on the moon, he said, "That's one small step for a man, one giant leap for mankind."

Since this historic landing on the moon, astronauts have continued to explore space by traveling there and by studying the data collected by satellites and other unmanned spacecraft. Through space exploration, astronauts and scientists have learned and continue to learn much about the universe beyond Earth.

Name: _____ Date: _____

Consequences and Implications

A3

What are the implications of space exploration? Support your answer.

Cause and Effect

A2

What is the effect of the Earth's gravitational pull on spacecraft during launch? During reentry? Support your answer with evidence from the text.

Sequencing

A1

Create a timeline of the history of space exploration as presented in the text.

THE EXPLORATION OF SPACE

Name: _____ Date: _____

Creative Synthesis

D3

Imagine you are an astronaut on the Apollo 8 spacecraft. Write a letter home describing the experience. Be sure to include plenty of details so the recipient of your letter feels like he or she was there with you.

Summarizing

D2

In three sentences or fewer, describe the different ways scientists and astronauts explore space.

Paraphrasing

D1

In your own words, explain what Neil Armstrong meant when he said, "That's one small step for a man, one giant leap for mankind."

THE EXPLORATION OF SPACE

Nonfiction 99

Name: _____ Date: _____

Graphic Ice Cream

Tim and Lauren, the owners of Crema, an ice cream shop in Raleigh, NC, surveyed their customers about their favorite ice cream flavors, gathered information about the number of customers on each day of the week, and asked their employees to keep track of how they spend their work hours. They then used different kinds of graphs to represent these data.

Over the period of one month, the Crema owners asked their customers to choose their favorite flavors from a list including chocolate, vanilla, strawberry, banana toffee, strawberry cheesecake, blueberry almond, chocolate raspberry, coffee almond, peach pecan, and caramel pecan. The results are presented in Table 1.

Table 1
Customers' Favorite Flavors

Ice Cream Flavor	Number of Customers' Favorite Flavor
Chocolate	120
Vanilla	65
Strawberry	85
Banana Toffee	190
Strawberry Cheesecake	275
Blueberry Almond	135
Chocolate Raspberry	200
Coffee Almond	95
Peach Pecan	150
Caramel Pecan	75

Tim and Lauren then decided to graph the data they had gathered from their customers. They chose to graph the favorite flavors on a bar graph. A bar graph shows the relationships between groups. On a bar graph, one bar is not affected by another. Bar graphs are a good way to show large differences in results from surveys. They also are excellent tools for determining trends. By using a bar graph to represent the data about customers' favorite flavors, Lauren and Tim will be better able to plan their purchases of ingredients. They will know which ingredients will be used more quickly based on the flavor preferences. The bar graph of Crema customers' favorite flavors is presented in Figure 1.

Figure 1. Favorite ice cream flavors.

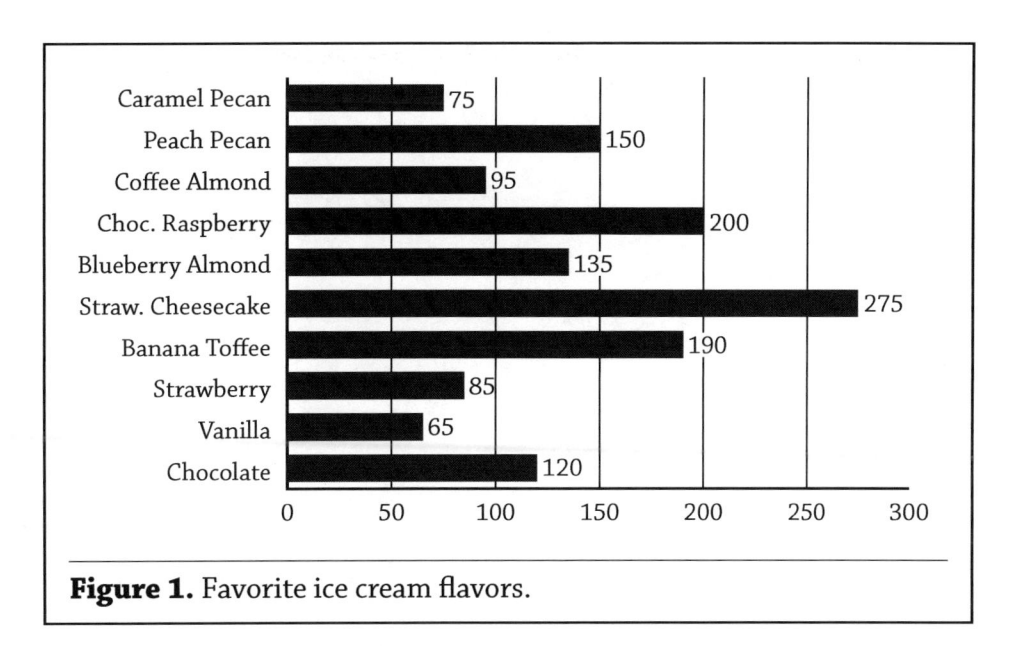

Flavor	Count
Caramel Pecan	75
Peach Pecan	150
Coffee Almond	95
Choc. Raspberry	200
Blueberry Almond	135
Straw. Cheesecake	275
Banana Toffee	190
Strawberry	85
Vanilla	65
Chocolate	120

After realizing how data can help them run their business more efficiently, Tim and Lauren decided to keep track of the number of customers coming to Crema on each day of the week. They were especially interested in Saturday and Sunday. They often wondered if they made or lost money by being open on the weekend. The results of their tracking are presented in Table 2.

Table 2
Number of Customers by Day

Day of the Week	Number of Customers
Monday	95
Tuesday	105
Wednesday	165
Thursday	210
Friday	275
Saturday	150
Sunday	45

Because the bar graph was helpful with comparing favorite flavors, the Crema owners decided to graph these data about customer attendance, too. However, instead of a bar graph, they chose to use a line graph. Line graphs track continuing data where one point is affected by another. With line graphs, there are points on a graph with x- and y-axis coordinates. Points are then joined by a line. Line graphs often are used to track rainfall, the average daily temperature, or, in the case of Crema, the daily number of customers. The line graph they used is presented in Figure 2.

Name: _____ Date: _____

Customers at Crema

[Line graph showing Number of Customers (0–300) by Days of the Week: Monday ~95, Tuesday ~100, Wednesday ~160, Thursday ~200, Friday ~275, Saturday ~160, Sunday ~45]

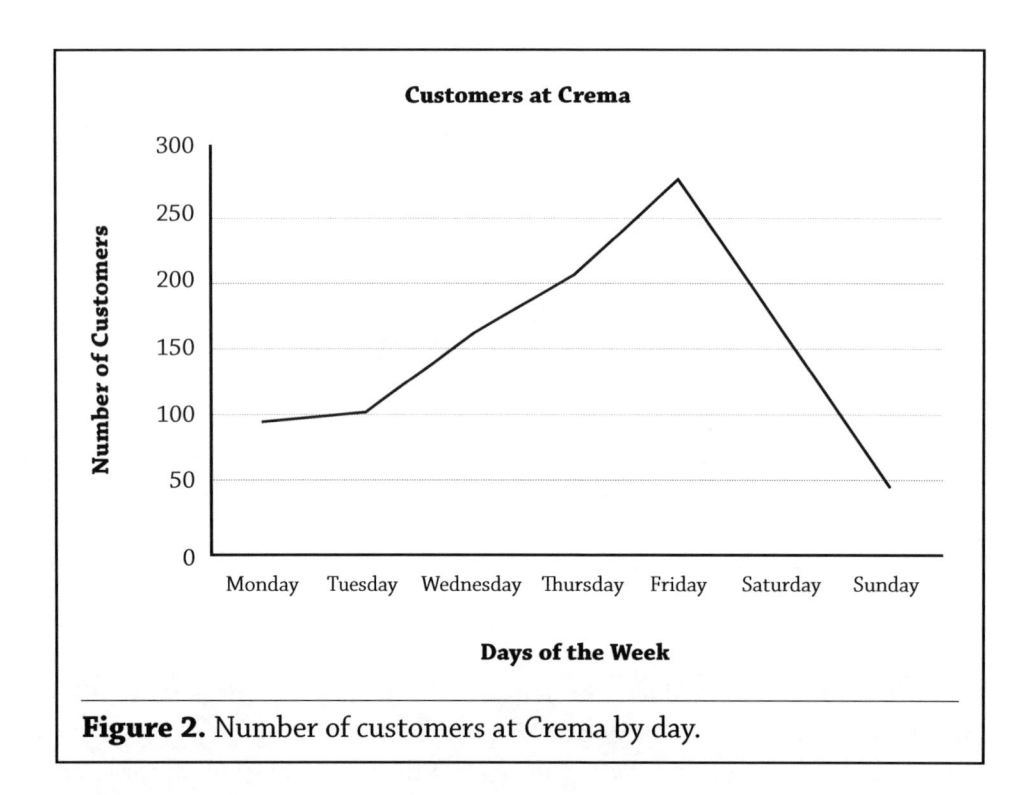

Figure 2. Number of customers at Crema by day.

Tim and Lauren analyzed the data to determine on what days they were most profitable. As they were thinking about money, they wondered how productive their employees were. They decided to ask their employees to keep track of how they spent their work hours. The results of this tracking are presented in Table 3.

Table 3
How Crema Employees Spend a Total Work Day (12 Hours)

Chore	Hours	Percentage of Work Day
Preparing Store to Open	1	8%
Taking Orders	3.5	30%
Preparing Orders	5	42%
Completing Transactions	1	8%
Reconciling Register	.5	4%
Closing	1	8%

The owners of Crema decided to use a circle, or pie, graph to display the data gathered from their employees. Pie graphs are particularly helpful when looking at how a part relates to a whole. In this case, Tim and Lauren wanted to see how the time spent on each chore related to the work day as a whole. The pie chart is presented in Figure 3.

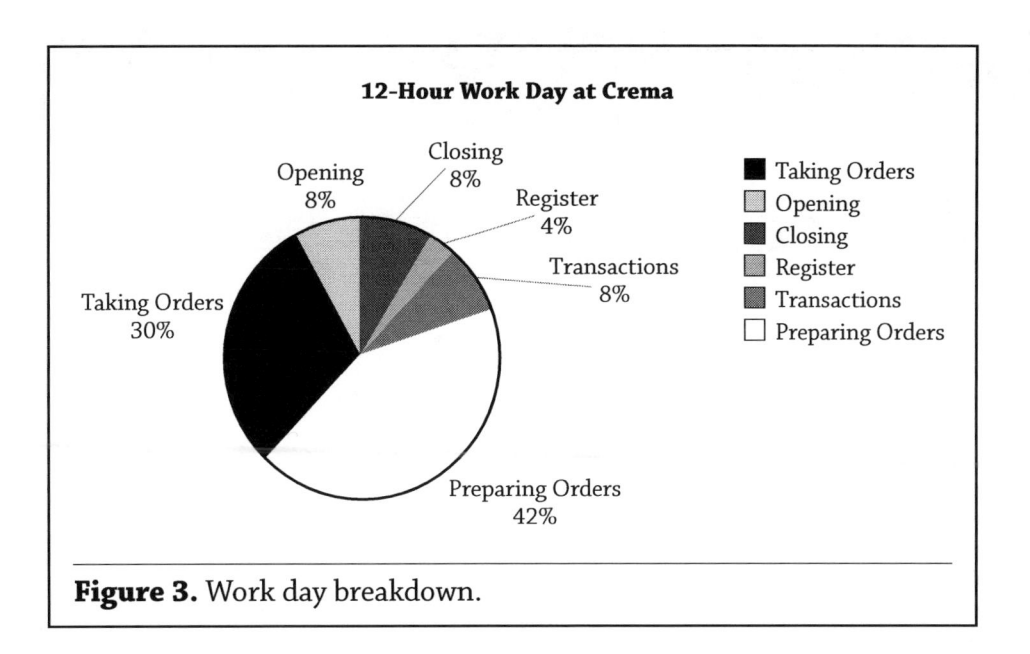

Name: _____   Date: _____

12-Hour Work Day at Crema

- Taking Orders 30%
- Opening 8%
- Closing 8%
- Register 4%
- Transactions 8%
- Preparing Orders 42%

Figure 3. Work day breakdown.

Name: _____ Date: _____

Generalizations

B3

Write at least three generalizations about using graphs to represent data.

Classifications

B2

Look at your list of details. Classify your list into the categories of bar, line, or pie graphs based on which type of graph would be most appropriate for each type of data. Use the definitions from the text to make your classification decisions.

Details

B1

List 15–20 different kinds of data that are often gathered or that could be gathered.

GRAPHIC ICE CREAM

104 Jacob's Ladder Reading Comprehension Program: GRADE 4

Name: _____ Date: _____

Main Idea, Theme, or Concept

C3

Main Idea: Why did the author title this selection "Graphic Ice Cream"? Use evidence from the text to support your answer.

Inference

C2

What inferences can you draw based on:
- the data and graph about customers' favorite flavors?
- the data and graph about daily customer counts?
- the data and graph about the use of employees' work hours?

Literary Elements

C1

How would you characterize the owners of Crema? Using details from the text to support your answer, describe the kind of business owners they are.

GRAPHIC ICE CREAM

Nonfiction 105

The Great Depression

The Great Depression began in the United States with the stock market crash of 1929. The Depression quickly spread throughout Europe and then the rest of the world.

Economists are divided over what caused the Great Depression. Some believe that at the end of the post-World War I building boom, consumer goods were flooding the market. The supply of goods was far exceeding demand, which caused the economic system to collapse. Others believe that it was a simple case of too many banks playing the stock market with depositors' money. A third theory contends that the Depression deepened because so many people were carrying debt before the crash, and when the crash occurred they simply stopped spending money, which crippled the capitalist market. Another theory blames the severity of the Depression on the extreme drought that struck the Midwest agricultural business during the summer of 1930. Finally, a fifth theory states that it was the collapse of foreign banks that took with it a large amount of U.S. wealth and destroyed the prospect of world trade that caused the Depression to become a Great Depression.

Regardless of the cause, the Great Depression was one of the saddest periods in U.S. history. During this time period from 1929 to 1941, Americans endured much hardship. In the Midwest, farmers experienced an intense drought that earned this agricultural area the name "Dust Bowl." During the summer of 1930, many Midwest farmers were forced to leave their lands because of dust storms that blew much of the soil away. The dust storms were caused by a failure to rotate crops and the exposure of soil by the removal of grass through plowing. With the drought, the soil dried out, became dust, and then blew away in black clouds. Much of the soil was lost in the Atlantic Ocean as it blew eastward. Many people in the Midwest suffered from dust pneumonia and malnutrition.

In other areas of the country, conditions were not any better. Unemployment rose from 5 million people without jobs in 1930 to 11 million people without jobs in 1931. A staggering 25% of Americans were unemployed. Many people lost their homes. Sadly, 20% of children were hungry and did not have proper clothing or houses. Many schools closed because they could not afford to stay open. Of young people between the ages of 16 and 24, 40% of them were neither in school nor working. Children wrote letters to the First Lady, Eleanor Roosevelt, begging her to help them find food, clothing, and shelter.

After his inauguration in 1933, President Franklin D. Roosevelt passed the New Deal legislation. The New Deal restructured the economy and increased government spending to stimulate demand within the market, create jobs, and provide relief for the poor and unemployed. However, in 1937, the American economy took another nosedive that further deepened the Great Depression. During the period of the Depression, most countries experienced political upheaval that allowed dictators like Hitler, Stalin, and Mussolini to rise to power, leading to the beginning of World War II in 1939.

Supplying materials and resources for troops to protect the world against Nazi Germany stimulated economies in Europe from 1937–1939, pulling these nations out of depression. In the U.S., jobs increased, people worked overtime to make up for lost wages, and Americans agreed to rations for the first time in support of the war effort. The President pushed for a large quantity of war supplies no matter what it cost the government. In the United States, the Great Depression ended in 1941 when America entered World War II.

Name: _____ Date: _____

Consequences and Implications

A3

What were the consequences of the Great Depression for children? Justify your answer with supporting details.

Cause and Effect

A2

What caused the end of the Great Depression in Europe? In America? Support your answer.

Sequencing

A1

List, in order, the events of the Great Depression as discussed in the text.

THE GREAT DEPRESSION

Name: _____ Date: _____

Generalizations

B3

Write at least three generalizations about your life today compared to the life of a child during the Great Depression.

Classifications

B2

Study your list. Classify your details into categories. You may not have a "miscellaneous" or "other" category.

Details

B1

List at least 25 things and/or privileges that you have today that you would not have had growing up during the Great Depression.

THE GREAT DEPRESSION

Nonfiction

It's Electric!

How much do you know about electricity? Electricity refers to the movement of charged particles within atoms. There are two kinds of charged particles: Electrons have a negative charge, and protons have a positive charge. Electrons are constantly orbiting the nucleus of an atom. When an electromotive force is applied through an energy source such as a battery or an outlet, the electrons will jump from nucleus to nucleus along the path of the force.

The rate at which electrons move is called *current*. Current is affected by resistance, which is related to the physical properties of the material through which electrons are moving. In materials with low resistance, like copper wire, electrons are easily persuaded to leave their original nucleus and travel to the next nucleus. Copper wire is a good conductor because electrons are easily conducted, or moved, along the path of the applied electromotive force. High resistance materials, such as rubber, make it nearly impossible for electrons to move from nucleus to nucleus. Rubber does not conduct electrons along the path of applied force. Because it does not allow conduction, rubber is called an *insulator*.

Another type of electricity is static electricity. With static electricity, the electrical particles are not moving; instead a charge has built up in something, like your body after rubbing your feet on carpet. When you rub your feet on the carpet, electrons are transferred from one object to the other. One object, either your feet or the carpet, ends up with extra electrons and a negative charge while the other object is positively charged because it has more protons. For the purposes of this example, let's say your feet are negatively charged and the carpet is positively charged. Then, you touch a neutral object, such as a doorknob, and experience a shock. The shock is actually a tiny lightning bolt that occurs when the extra negatively charged electrons are transferred to the neutrally charged doorknob. The electrons in your body are attracted to the protons in the doorknob and "jump" toward them. At the same time, the electrons already in the doorknob move as far away from the new electrons as possible. In the case of electricity, opposites attract.

Ancient Greeks were familiar with static electricity. They discovered the shocking characteristics of jumping electrons when they rubbed objects on fur. However, moving electricity produced by the application of an electromotive force was not discovered until much later. Many people believe Benjamin Franklin discovered electricity. Although this point is debatable, it can be said without doubt that Benjamin Franklin discovered that lightning is a form of electricity through his famous kite-flying experiment. In this experiment, Franklin tied a key to the end of a wet kite string. Then, he flew the kite during a lightning storm. When the lightning struck the key, he felt a spark on his finger and he knew that lightning was a form of electricity.

Thomas Edison is known as the inventor who was first able to capture electricity to produce light. He invented the light bulb and first demonstrated this invention on December 31, 1879 in Menlo Park, NJ. During this demonstration, he said, "We will make electricity so cheap that only the rich will burn candles."

Today, electricity is everywhere. There are lights in our houses, our schools, along our streets, and in our cars. Electricity even runs through our computers, our car engines, our televisions, our radios, and our video games.

Name: _____ Date: _____

Generalizations

B3 Based on your list and your classifications, write at least three generalizations about the use of electricity.

Classifications

B2 Look at your list of examples. Classify each example into categories. You may not have a "miscellaneous" or "other" category.

Details

B1 List as many examples of the use of electricity as you can in 2 minutes. (You should have at least 25 examples.)

IT'S ELECTRIC!

Name: _____ Date: _____

Creative Synthesis

D3

Invent a new way to use electricity. Create an advertisement to sell your new invention to an audience of your choice (your classmates, your teachers, your parents, your city, or another audience). You may use illustrations.

Summarizing

D2

In five sentences or fewer, summarize what happens when you rub your feet on the carpet and then touch a doorknob.

Paraphrasing

D1

In your own words, restate what Thomas Edison meant when he said, "We will make electricity so cheap that only the rich will burn candles."

IT'S ELECTRIC!

Nonfiction

The Metric System vs. the U.S. Customary System

The metric system and the U.S. customary system are both systems of measurement. So, what is the difference between them and why are there two different systems? In today's global society, wouldn't it be easier if the whole world used the same system?

Elements of the metric system date back to the reign of Louis XVI in France during the 18th century. In 1791, after the French Revolution, the metric system was adopted by the French as the official system of measurement. The goals of the new metric system were to develop a single unit for physical quantity and to create a measurement system that did not require the use of conversion factors. Specifically, all measurements of length are in meters, measurements of liquid are in liters, and measurements of weight are in grams. All three types of measurement use a common set of prefixes that are related to each other by powers of 10. For example, a decameter is 10 meters, a hectometer is 100 meters, and a kilometer is 1,000 meters. Conversely, a decimeter is 1/10 of a meter, a centimeter is 1/100 of a meter, and millimeter is 1/1000 of a meter. There are no conversion factors required to switch among these different representations of the measurement of length. Time is the only unit of measurement that is not unified by the metric system. Time still requires conversion factors to switch among days, hours, minutes, and seconds.

The U.S. customary system can be traced back to the Roman system of measurement. It is based on the Imperial System, which was used by Great Britain until 1995. Today, the United States is the only country that has not converted to the metric system from the customary system, even though the Omnibus Trade and Competitiveness Act of 1988 stated that the metric system is the preferred system for industry and trade. In the United States, the metric system is most commonly used by the military, medical field, and scientific realms. The customary system is used in most other instances. The customary system measures length in inches, feet, yards, and miles; measures general volume in cubic inches, cubic feet, and cubic yards; measures liquid volume in fluid ounces, cups, pints, quarts, and gallons; and measures weight in ounces, pounds,

Name: _____ Date: _____

Customary System			Metric System		
From	Multiply by	To get	From	Multiply by	To get
feet	12	inches	kilometers	1000	meters
pounds	16	ounces	grams	1000	milligrams
quarts	4	cups	liters	10	deciliters

Figure 1. Converting units in the customary system vs. the metric system.

and tons. The customary system requires conversion factors to convert units. For example, to convert feet into yards, you must know that there are 3 feet in one yard. You then would divide the total number of feet by three to determine the total number of yards. Similarly, to convert cups into quarts, you have to know that there are 4 cups in a quart.

The chart in Figure 1 shows the conversion factors needed for the customary system compared to conversion of measurement units within the metric system.

Which system do you think is easier?

Name: _____ Date: _____

Consequences and Implications

A3

What are the implications of the United States being the only country that has not officially converted to the metric system? Justify your answer.

Cause and Effect

A2

What caused the French to adopt the metric system after the French Revolution? Support your answer.

Sequencing

A1

List the elements of the metric system and the U.S. customary system in the order in which they were discussed in the text.

THE METRIC SYSTEM VS. THE U.S. CUSTOMARY SYSTEM

Name: _____ Date: _____

Main Idea, Theme, or Concept

C3

Theme: Does the overall theme of the text support the use of the U.S. customary system? Why or why not?

Inference

C2

What inferences can be made from the chart in Figure 1? Support your answer with details from the text.

Literary Elements

C1

Imagine a conversation between an American and a French person about the use of the metric system vs. the customary system. Choose one character from this scenario. Describe your chosen character's point of view on this topic. Use details to support your description.

THE METRIC SYSTEM VS. THE U.S. CUSTOMARY SYSTEM

Nonfiction   117

Appendix A

Pre- and Postassessments and Exemplars

Appendix A contains the pre- and postassessment readings and answer forms, as well as a rubric for scoring the assessments. The preassessment should be administered before any work with *Jacob's Ladder* is conducted. After all readings and questions have been answered, the postassessment can be given to track student improvement on the ladder skill sets. Included in this appendix are example answers for both the pre- and postassessments. The answers are taken from student responses given during the piloting of this curriculum.

Name: _____ Date: _____

Preassessment

The Old Woman and the Physician
Originally told by Aesop

An old woman, having lost the use of her eyes, called in a physician to heal them and made this bargain with him in the presence of witnesses: that if he should cure her blindness, he should receive from her a sum of money; but if her infirmity remained, she should give him nothing. This agreement being made, the physician, time after time, applied his salve to her eyes, and on every visit took something away, stealing all of her property little by little. And when he had got all she had, he healed her and demanded the promised payment. The old woman, when she recovered her sight and saw none of her goods in her house, would give him nothing. The physician insisted on his claim, and as she still refused, summoned her before the judge. The old woman, standing up in the court, argued: "This man here speaks the truth in what he says; for I did promise to give him a sum of money if I should recover my sight: but if I continued blind, I was to give him nothing. Now he declares that I am healed. I on the contrary affirm that I am still blind; for when I lost the use of my eyes, I saw in my house various chattels and valuable goods: but now, though he swears I am cured of my blindness, I am not able to see a single thing in it."

Name: _____ Date: _____

Preassessment: Questions

Read and answer each question, using evidence from the reading to support your ideas.

1. What do you think the judge will do in this case? Why? Provide evidence from the story to defend your answer.

   _____
   _____
   _____
   _____
   _____
   _____

2. What does the old woman mean when she says, "but now, though he swears I am cured of my blindness, I am not able to see a single thing"? Provide evidence from the story to defend your answer.

   _____
   _____
   _____
   _____
   _____
   _____

Name: _____ Date: _____

Preassessment: Questions, *continued.*

3. What is the moral of this story? Give a reason why you think so.

   _____
   _____
   _____
   _____
   _____
   _____

4. Create a new title for this story. Give a reason why your title is better than the original title.

   _____
   _____
   _____
   _____
   _____
   _____
   _____

Name: _____ Date: _____

Postassessment

The King and the Shirt

By Leo Tolstoy

A king once fell ill. "I will give half my kingdom to the man who can cure me," he said. All of his wise men gathered together to decide how the king could be cured. But no one knew. Only one of the wise men said what he thought would cure the king. "If you can find a happy man, take his shirt, put it on the king—and the king will be cured." The king sent his emissaries to search for a happy man. They traveled far and wide throughout his whole kingdom, but they could not find a happy man. There was no one who was completely satisfied: if a man was rich he was ailing; if he was healthy he was poor; if he was rich and healthy he had a bad wife; or if he had children they were bad—everyone had something to complain of. Finally, late one night, the king's son was passing by a poor little hut and he heard someone say: "Now, God be praised, I have finished my work, I have eaten my fill, and I can lie down and sleep! What more could I want?" The king's son rejoiced and gave orders that the man's shirt be taken and carried to the king, and that the man be given as much money as he wanted. The emissaries went in to take the man's shirt, but the happy man was so poor that he had no shirt.

Name: _____ Date: _____

Postassessment: Questions

Read and answer each question, using evidence from the reading to support your ideas.

1. What do you think will happen next since the happy man has no shirt? Why? Provide evidence from the story to defend your answer.

   _____
   _____
   _____
   _____
   _____
   _____

2. Why do you think the man without a shirt was happy when no one else was? Provide evidence from the story to defend your answer.

   _____
   _____
   _____
   _____
   _____
   _____

Name: _____ Date: _____

Postassessment: Questions, *continued.*

3. What is the moral of this story? Give a reason why you think so.

   _____

   _____

   _____

   _____

   _____

   _____

4. Create a new title for this story. Give a reason why your title is better than the original title.

   _____

   _____

   _____

   _____

   _____

   _____

Name: _____ Date: _____

Assessment Scoring Rubric

Question	Points 0	1	2	3	4
1 Implications and Consequences (Ladder A)	Provides no response or response is inappropriate to the task demand	Limited, vague, inaccurate; rewords the prompt or copies from text	Response is accurate and makes sense but does not adequately address all components of the question or provide rationale from text	Response is accurate; answers all parts of the question; provides a rationale that justifies answer	Response is well written, specific, insightful; answers all parts of the questions, offers substantial support, and incorporates evidence from the text
2 Inference (Ladder C)	Provides no response or response is inappropriate to the task demand	Limited, vague, inaccurate; rewords the prompt or copies from text	Accurate response but literal interpretation with no support from the text	Interpretive response with limited support from the text	Insightful, interpretive, well-written response with substantial support from the text
3 Theme/Generalization (Ladders B and C)	Provides no response or response is inappropriate to the task demand	Limited, vague, inaccurate; rewords the prompt or copies from text	Literal description of the story without explaining the theme; no reasons why	Valid, interpretive response with limited reasoning from the text	Insightful, interpretive response with substantial justification or reasoning
4 Creative Synthesis (Ladder D)	Provides no response or response is inappropriate to the task demand	Limited, vague, inaccurate; rewords the prompt or copies from text	Appropriate but literal title with no attempt to support	Interpretive title with limited reasoning or justification	Insightful title, interpretive, and extensive justification or reasoning

Example Answers
Preassessment: The Old Woman and the Physician

Note. These answers are based on student responses and teacher ratings from field trials conducted by the Center for Gifted Education. The answers have not been changed from the original student response.

1. What do you think the judge will do in this case? Why? Provide evidence from the story to defend your answer.

    1-point responses might include:

    - Make the woman pay because she is lying.
    - I think that the judge will think that the old woman is innocent because she is still blind.
    - Tell her to get glasses or eye contacts.

    2-point responses might include:

    - I think the judge will go to the Physician's house and look for the stolen goods.
    - I think the judge will make him give her goods back to her or else be put in jail for selling her stuff.
    - The judge will not make her pay the Physician.

    3-point responses might include:

    - I think the judge will say the Physician is guilty because the woman said, "he swore he cured me but I can't see anything in my home."
    - I think the judge will say the woman won the case because the Physician stole everything the woman owned and wants more.
    - I think the judge will find the man guilty because when the old lady was going blind she could see valuable stuff but when she was cured she couldn't see valuable stuff.

    4-point responses might include:

    - I think the judge will trick the physician. The judge will say she does not have to pay until she can see her things. When the physician brings them back he will be arrested for stealing.

Appendix A

- I think the judge will find out the man stole little by little because before she went blind she saw various chattels but when she went blind and got better there was nothing left.
- The judge will make the Physician give back everything he took and not make the old woman pay him for curing her because he was greedy and stole her valuable goods and still demanded payment.

2. What does the old woman mean when she says, "but now, though he swears I am cured of my blindness, I am not able to see a single thing"? Provide evidence from the story to defend your answer.

1-point responses might include:

- The Physician says she is cured but she says she is not able to see a thing.
- The woman means she can't see anything because she is still blind.
- I think she means that someone tried to fix her eyes but it didn't work because she still couldn't see anything.

2-point responses might include:

- I think the old woman says that because she thinks the Physician stole all her valuable goods.
- She says that because while he was curing her he stole all of her things.
- She means she is cured but can't see her goods.

3-point responses might include:

- The old woman means that she still can't see even though she has been cured because there is nothing in her house to see.
- The old lady means that she can't see any of her possessions. That is because all of her possessions are missing.
- She can't see anything in her house because there isn't anything in her house.

4-point responses might include:

- She means she can see because the physician cured her but does not have anything to look at in her house. I think this because

> the story says every time the doctor gave her medicine he took something.
> - She means even though she can see again, she still can't see any of her goods in her house because the Physician stole them all.
> - The old woman means that she had valuable goods in her house before she went blind but when she got her sight back they were all gone so she couldn't see them anymore.

3. What is the moral of this story? Give a reason why you think so.

   1-point responses might include:
   - I think it is all about money.
   - If you're blind, stick with it.
   - The man speaks the truth.

   2-point responses might include:
   - The moral is the Physician stole all her goods while the woman was blind.
   - The moral of this story is the Physician took all of her things.
   - The moral of the story is that the old woman is blind and didn't know that her stuff was stolen and when she was cured she did not have anything.

   3-point responses might include:
   - The moral of the story is never steal because it is wrong.
   - Don't trust someone that you don't know when you are blind, you may get something stolen.
   - The moral of the story is don't promise because you could get in big trouble.

   4-point responses might include:
   - You should not trick someone because the person you tricked can find out everything even if they are blind, deaf, or others. My reason is that the blind woman found out the Physician stole her things and then did not pay him for curing her.
   - The moral of the story is don't be greedy. The Physician stole all the old woman's stuff and tried to make her pay him and now he has to go to court and probably won't end up with anything.

- The moral of the story is to be careful who you trust, because the old woman trusted the Physician she thought was good and he stole from her.

4. Create a new title for this story. Give a reason why your title is better than the original title.

1-point responses might include:

- The Physician.
- Two People Going Blind because two people go blind.
- The Blinding Eye.

2-point responses might include:

- The Old Blind Woman and the Physician. My title is better than the other title because it talks about a blind old woman and a Physician.
- Lady and the Eye Doctor. Some people don't know what a Physician is so you can call him an eye doctor.
- The Woman and the Thief. The original title is boring.

3-point responses might include:

- Is She Blind? Because the story is trying to figure out if she's still blind.
- The Physician Bandit, because he took her stuff.
- Watch Out for the Physician. I would title it this so it could warn people about the robber physician.

4-point responses might include:

- The title I would pick is Pay If You Have To. I picked this title because she has to pay if he fixed her eyes. She promised to pay and you should keep promises.
- The Blind Woman and the Sneaky Physician. I think my title is better because it tells that the Physician took valuable things while the woman was blind. The physician was a liar and a cheat.
- The Woman and the Greedy Physician. I think my title is better than the original because the Physician stole the woman's belongings and wanted the money she said she'd give him money if he cured her too.

Example Answers
Postassessment: The King and the Shirt

Note. These answers are based on student responses and teacher ratings from field trials conducted by the Center for Gifted Education. The answers have not been changed from the original student response.

1. What do you think will happen next since the happy man has no shirt? Why? Provide evidence from the story to defend your answer.

   1-point responses might include:
   - The poor man has to have a shirt.
   - The king's men took his shirt from him.
   - He will have no shirt.

   2-point responses might include:
   - The king will die.
   - I think the king will get very sick.
   - The king will learn how to be happy.

   3-point responses might include:
   - He did not have a shirt to give to the king so the king remained uncured.
   - I think that since the happy man has no shirt they will give him one to wear for a couple weeks and then take it to the king.
   - I think since the happy man had no shirt they should find a new cure to help the king because there is no way to take a shirt from someone who doesn't have a shirt.

   4-point responses might include:
   - I think since the happy man had no shirt the king won't be cured. I know that because it says in the story "If you can find a happy man take his shirt, put it on the king—and the king will be cured" and the happy man has no shirt so the king won't be cured.

Appendix A

- The king will find out that you don't have to be rich to be happy since the poor man was happy without a shirt the king can be happy without a shirt too.
- I think they will keep searching for a happy man's shirt because they searched far and wide for a long time before so they'll probably keep looking.

2. Why do you think the man without a shirt was happy when no one else was? Provide evidence from the story to defend your answer.

1-point responses might include:

- He only had to get a shirt and then he could get all the money he needs.
- He was used to not having a shirt.
- I think the man was happy because the king's son said I will give you money.

2-point responses might include:

- He was happy because he could sleep.
- He was happy because he had all his work done.
- He was happy because he didn't complain.

3-point responses might include:

- He had food and a home so he was grateful for what he had.
- He had all he wanted. The man said, "What more could I want?"
- I think the poor man was happy because he didn't want anything.

4-point responses might include:

- I think the man with no shirt was happy because he was content with what he had. He said he had finished his work, eaten his fill and he could now rest.
- I think he was happy because he was thankful for what he had. It even says in the story that he was thanking God for what had happened and what he had.
- The man was happy because he didn't care that he was poor. He didn't complain like everyone else because he only cared about the important things.

3. What is the moral of this story? Give a reason why you think so.

   1-point responses might include:
   - What more could I want?
   - The moral is always wear a shirt.
   - Poor people don't always have shirts.

   2-point responses might include:
   - Trying to cure the king. They are trying to find a happy man with a shirt.
   - The moral of the story is that the king is ill and he needs to be cured.
   - The king stole shirts and he shouldn't.

   3-point responses might include:
   - I think the moral of this story was that it is hard to find someone who is really happy because many have many complaints and things that make them mad or sad.
   - Be happy with what you already have because the man didn't have a lot.
   - You don't need to be rich to be happy.

   4-point responses might include:
   - I think the moral of the story is to be happy with what you have. In the story the happy man was thankful for what he had. He was done working, eating and was going to go to sleep so he was happy.
   - Even if you are poor and don't even have a shirt you can still be happy because the poor man with no shirt was the only man that they could find that was happy.
   - You don't have to be rich to be happy. The only happy man they could find was so poor he didn't have a shirt.

4. Create a new title for this story. Give a reason why your title is better than the original title.

   1-point responses might include:
   - A Lot of Trouble.

Appendix A **133**

- The Poor Man Gets Rich.
- The Long Journey.

2-point responses might include:

- The Ill King and the Very Poor Man because it sounds better.
- <u>Finding a Happy Man's Shirt</u>. The original title said, <u>The King and the Shirt</u> and the shirt is not a main character.
- <u>The Never Cured King</u> because I think it sounds exciting.

3-point responses might include:

- <u>The Cure</u>. Because the king is looking for a cure.
- <u>The King's Happy Man</u>. I think this title is better because in the story the King was sick so he searched for a happy man.
- <u>The Man Who Was Always Happy</u> because the story talks more about him than the ill king.

4-point responses might include:

- <u>Be Thankful For What You Have</u>. I think it is a better title because the story talks about all the people who should be thankful for what they have. Like the rich man who was sick and the healthy man who was poor.
- <u>How to Be Happy</u>. Because the story was mainly about why the happy man was happy. To be happy you should be thankful for what you have.
- <u>The Only Happy Man</u>. I think this is a better title because they traveled far and wide through the whole kingdom and they could only find one happy man. All the others were not totally happy.

Appendix B

Record-Keeping Forms/Documents

Appendix B contains four record-keeping forms and documents:

- *Brainstorming/Answer Sheet*: This should be given to students for completion after reading a selection so that they may jot ideas or questions about the selection they read prior to participating in discussion. The purpose of this sheet is to capture students' thoughts and ideas generated after individually reading a text. This sheet serves as a guide for student preparedness so that the student is ready to share ideas in group discussion.

- *Assessment/Response Form*: This form may be used by the student as an answer sheet for a given ladder. The student may self-assess his or her work on the ladder in the form of a numerical score. The teacher may also provide a numerical form for feedback. In addition, there is space for both the student and the teacher to write comments about the student's work on the ladder.

- *Reflection Page*: This form may be completed by the student after group or class discussion on the readings. The reflection page is designed as a metacognitive approach to help students reflect on their strengths and weaknesses and to promote process skills. After discussion, students use the reflection page to record new ideas that were generated by others' comments and ideas.

- *Classroom Diagnostic Forms*: These forms are for teachers and are designed to aid them in keeping track of the progress and skill mastery of their students. With these charts, teachers can record student progress in relation to each ladder skill within a genre and select additional ladders and story selections based on student needs.

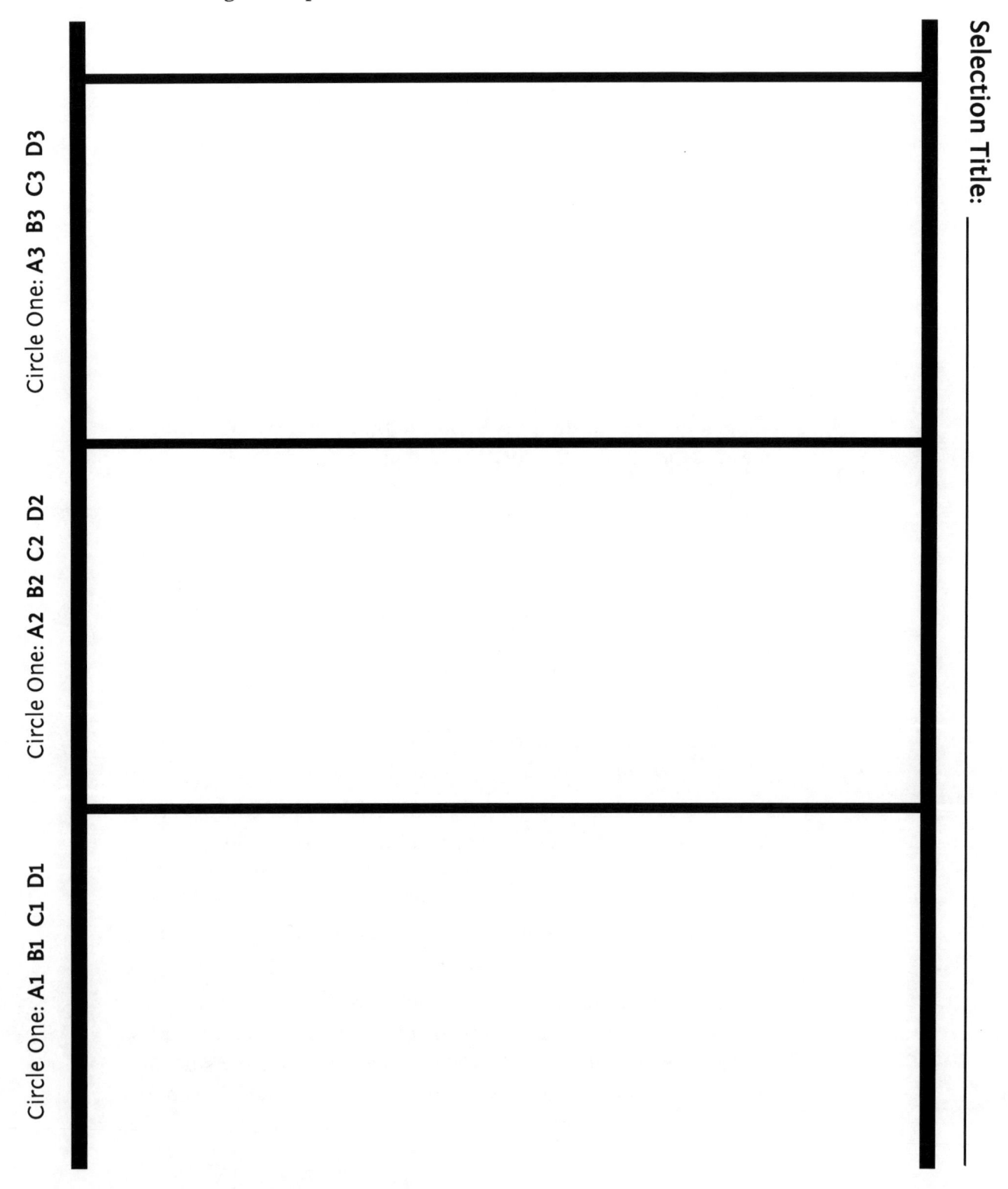

Name: _____ Date: _____

Brainstorming/Answer Sheet

Use this form to brainstorm thoughts and ideas about the readings and ladder questions before discussing with a partner.

Selection Title: _____

Circle One: **A3 B3 C3 D3**

Circle One: **A2 B2 C2 D2**

Circle One: **A1 B1 C1 D1**

136 Jacob's Ladder Reading Comprehension Program: GRADE 4

Name: _____ Date: _____

Assessment/Response Form

Use this form as an answer sheet. Both you and your teacher may also assess your work on this page.

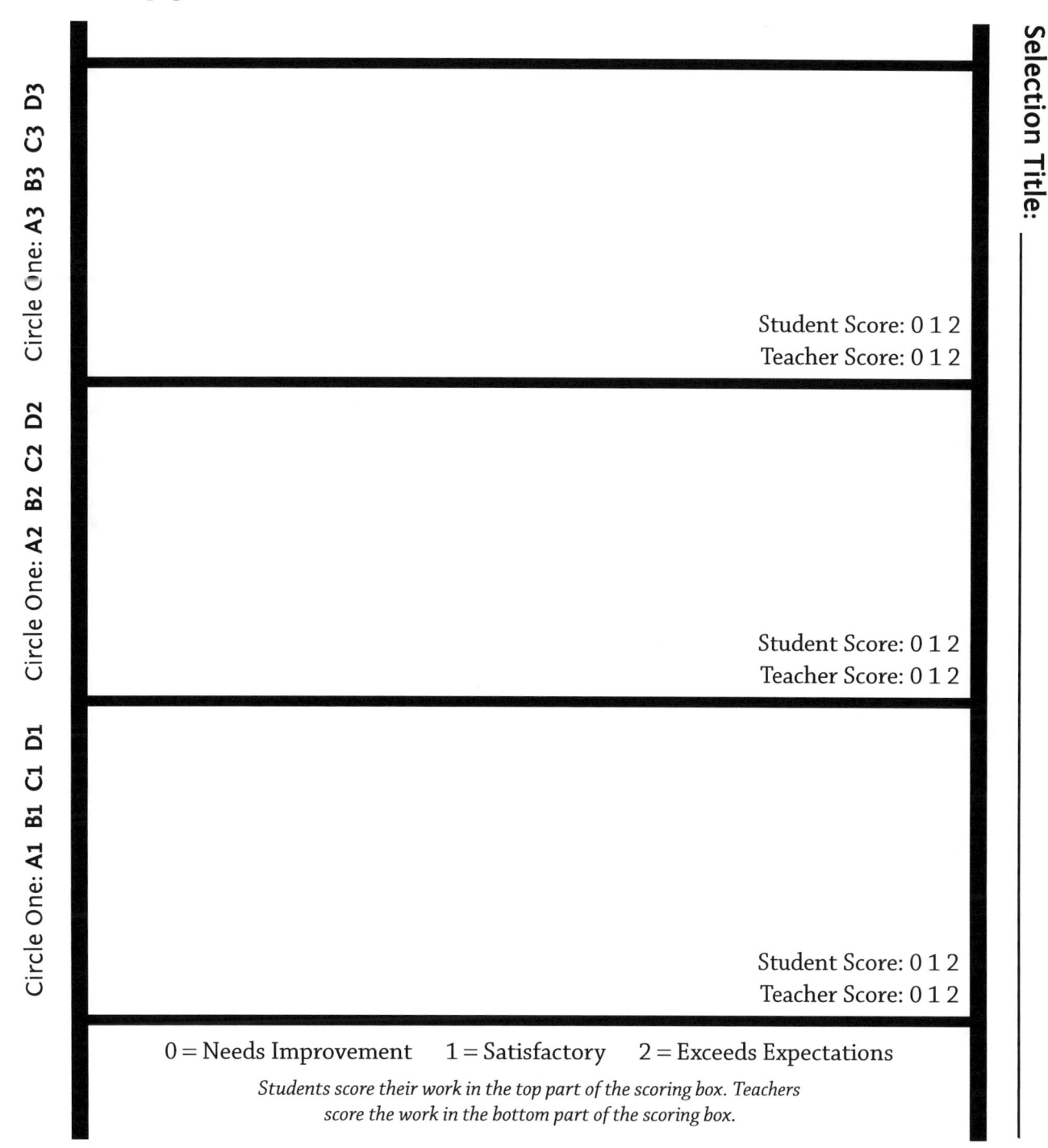

Circle One: **A3 B3 C3 D3**

Student Score: 0 1 2
Teacher Score: 0 1 2

Circle One: **A2 B2 C2 D2**

Student Score: 0 1 2
Teacher Score: 0 1 2

Circle One: **A1 B1 C1 D1**

Student Score: 0 1 2
Teacher Score: 0 1 2

0 = Needs Improvement   1 = Satisfactory   2 = Exceeds Expectations

Students score their work in the top part of the scoring box. Teachers score the work in the bottom part of the scoring box.

Selection Title: _____

Student Comments: Is there anything you would like your teacher to know about your work on this reading?

Appendix B   137

Name: _____ Date: _____

My Reflection on Today's Reading and Discussion

Selection Title: _____

What I did well:

_____
_____
_____
_____

What I learned:

_____
_____
_____
_____

New ideas I have after discussion:

_____
_____
_____
_____

Next time I need to:

_____
_____
_____
_____

Classroom Diagnostic Form
Short Stories

Use this document to record student completion of ladder sets with the assessment of work.

0 = Needs Improvement   1 = Satisfactory   2 = Exceeds Expectations

Student Name	Androcles C	Androcles D	Arachne and Athena B	Arachne and Athena C	Rumpel-Stilts-Ken A	Rumpel-Stilts-Ken C	The Three Painters B	The Three Painters C	The Fox and the Cat B	The Fox and the Cat C	The Lost Wig A	The Lost Wig C

Appendix B

Classroom Diagnostic Form
Short Stories

Use this document to record student completion of ladder sets with the assessment of work.
0 = Needs Improvement   1 = Satisfactory   2 = Exceeds Expectations

Student Name	Finding the Writer Inside C	Finding the Writer Inside D	The Myth of Athena A	The Myth of Athena D	The Myth of Heracles A	The Myth of Heracles D	Theseus and the Minotaur B	Theseus and the Minotaur D

Classroom Diagnostic Form
Poetry

Use this document to record student completion of ladder sets with the assessment of work.

0 = Needs Improvement   1 = Satisfactory   2 = Exceeds Expectations

Student Name	I Am Autumn		13 Ways of Looking at a Rose		Sweet Summer		My Shadow		After the Winter		Travel	
	C	C	B	C	B	C	B	C	B	C	B	C

Appendix B   **141**

Classroom Diagnostic Form
Poetry

Use this document to record student completion of ladder sets with the assessment of work.

0 = Needs Improvement   1 = Satisfactory   2 = Exceeds Expectations

Student Name	Saving Words		Dubstep		Approach of Winter	
	A	C	B	C	B	C

Classroom Diagnostic Form
Nonfiction

Use this document to record student completion of ladder sets with the assessment of work.

0 = Needs Improvement   1 = Satisfactory   2 = Exceeds Expectations

Student Name	The American Revolutionary War			The Exploration of Space			Graphic Ice Cream			The Great Depression			It's Electric!			The Metric System vs. the U.S. Customary System		
	C	D		A	D		B	C		A	B		B	D		A	C	

Appendix B

Answer Key

This key includes example answers for all ladder questions. Sample answers were generated to illustrate the skills students should be mastering. However, because the questions are open-ended and designed to promote discussion, these answers should only be used as a guide. Variations and original thought should be valued and rewarded.

Short Stories

These are suggested answers only. Answers will vary.

Androcles

Ladder Set C

C1. Androcles is a kind, brave, and caring person. Once he realized that the lion was not going to attack him, he was not afraid of the lion anymore. Instead of running away, he cared enough to find out what was wrong with the lion. He realized the lion was another living creature that deserved care and compassion. He was kind to the lion by taking care of him.

C2. The lion did not eat Androcles because Androcles was a friend. Androcles took care of the lion's paw; without the help of Androcles the lion probably would not have survived because it would have been attacked by an enemy or killed by an infection from the wound. I was not surprised the lion spared Androcles because animals often are as loyal as or more loyal than people.

C3. Answers will vary. An example might be, "Be kind to others and they will be kind to you" because Androcles helped the lion who returned the favor by not eating him.

Ladder Set D

D1. The Lion recognized Androcles as the person who helped him when his paw was hurt. He knew he could not hurt someone who had been so kind to him. He decided he would rather go hungry than to harm a friend. The emperor was so impressed that he demanded Androcles tell him why the lion did not eat him. The emperor was amazed at the friendship and decided to free both Androcles and the lion.

D2. You never know when a kindness toward another will be repaid. (Support: Androcles didn't foresee a situation for the lion to repay the favor, but when such a situation did arise, the lion was quick to treat Androcles as he had been treated.)

D3. Answers will vary. The fable should be short, have a moral, and be related to the main idea identified by the student in the answer to D2.

Arachne and Athena

Ladder Set B

B1. Answers will vary. Some examples might include: She will not be able to walk around town without fear of getting stepped on; she will not be able to sell her cloth; she will not be able to weave cloth, only webs; she will not be able to talk; she will have to eat flies.

B2. Answers will vary. Some examples using the list above might include: relationships with others, livelihood, or lifestyle.

B3. Answers will vary. An example using the list and categories above might be: "Change can be positive or negative."

Ladder Set C

C1.:

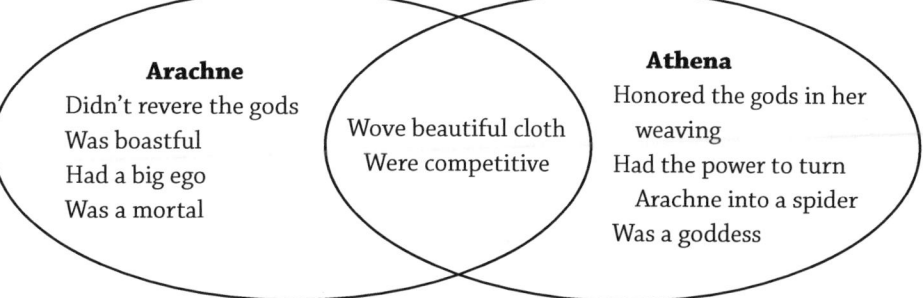

Arachne
Didn't revere the gods
Was boastful
Had a big ego
Was a mortal

Wove beautiful cloth
Were competitive

Athena
Honored the gods in her weaving
Had the power to turn Arachne into a spider
Was a goddess

C2. Arachne tried to outweave Athena because she thought she was a better weaver and she wanted to prove it. Also, Arachne did not respect the gods and goddesses, including Athena. Arachne thought she could prove the gods and goddesses were no different or better than mortals.

C3. We learn that we should not be egotistical. We should not think we are better at a skill than everyone else, but should appreciate everyone's talents.

Rumpel-Stilts-Ken

Ladder Set A

A1. 1. The miller told the king that his daughter could spin gold out of straw; 2. The hobgoblin (dwarf) spun the first batch of straw into gold in exchange for the miller's daughter's necklace; 3. The hobgoblin (dwarf) spun the second batch of straw into gold in exchange for the miller's daughter's ring; 4. The miller's daughter promised the hobgoblin (dwarf) her firstborn child if he would spin straw into gold for a third time so that the king would marry her; 5. The king married the miller's daughter and she became the queen; 6. The queen learned the hobgoblin's (dwarf's) name from a messenger and was able to avoid giving her child away to him.

A2. The hobgoblin (dwarf) "dashed his foot in a rage" when the queen said his name because she had found out his name. This meant that she would not have to give him her firstborn child.

A3.:
- If the hobgoblin (dwarf) had not spun the straw into gold for the miller's daughter, her life would have been very different. The king told her that she had to spin the straw into gold before morning, "as you love your life"; that sounds like a death threat. She was left alone in a chamber with the door locked, so she might have been left alone to die there.
- If the miller's daughter had not promised her firstborn child to the hobgoblin (dwarf) for spinning the straw into gold, he might not have spun the straw for her. The king would not have married her because she did not spin the straw.
- If the messenger had not heard the hobgoblin (dwarf) singing his name, the queen probably would not have figured out his name. She would have to give her firstborn child to him.

Ladder Set C

C1. Answers will vary. Sample response: The miller's daughter was shrewd and clever. The narrator said that she was shrewd and clever. Her actions throughout the story proved that she was. For example, she persuaded the hobgoblin (dwarf) to spin the straw into gold for her by promising him various things.

C2. Answers will vary. Sample response: If given the opportunity, the hobgoblin (dwarf) might have taken "all the wealth of the kingdom" instead of insisting that the queen figure out his name in order to keep her baby. If he had taken the money, he would be a wealthy man.

C3. Answers will vary. Sample response: One theme might be "greed makes people do ridiculous things." The evidence is that the king wants gold so badly that he was willing to threaten the miller's daughter with death if she couldn't spin the straw into gold. Other evidence is that the king married the miller's daughter as a result of his greed.

The Three Painters

Ladder Set B

B1. Answers will vary. Some examples might include:
- The three painters: not rich; talented; resourceful; disagreeable; competitive; eager to do well
- King Leopold: generous; resourceful; caring; worked on behalf of the best interests of his kingdom; eager to do well

B2. Answers will vary. An example is shown below:

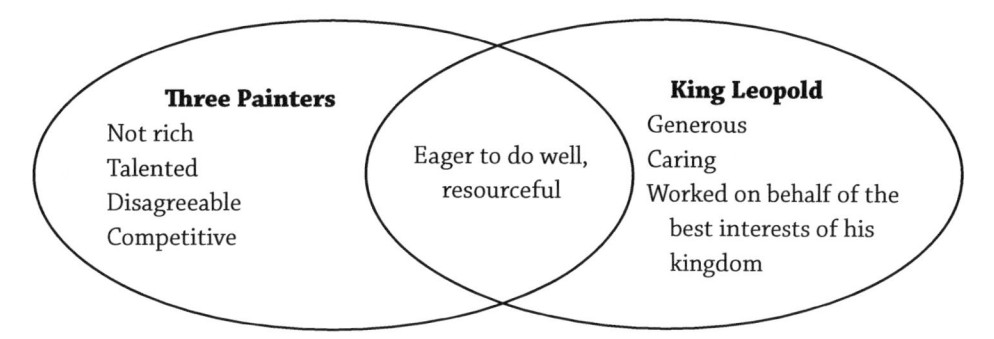

Three Painters
Not rich
Talented
Disagreeable
Competitive

Eager to do well, resourceful

King Leopold
Generous
Caring
Worked on behalf of the best interests of his kingdom

B3. Answers will vary.

Ladder Set C

C1. One theme is that working together as a team is often more productive than working against each other. The evidence is in this sentence: "The three brothers learned to put their differences behind them, and they learned that they worked best when they worked together as one mind."

Another theme is that it is important to honor your obligations, or there may be consequences. The evidence is in these sentences said by King Leopold: "For your actions against the kingdom, you three shall be stripped of your title. You are no longer allowed in the palace. In addition, I am exiling you three from the kingdom of Norman. You are no longer to return to this kingdom ever again."

C2. If given the opportunity, the three painters might live their lives differently. The evidence that supports my position is in this sentence: "The three brothers learned to put their differences behind them, and they learned that they worked best when they worked together as one mind." This tells me that they learned their actions had not served them well, so they would do things differently in the future.

C3. King Leopold is generous. The evidence is in this sentence: "Because King Leopold was generous, the three brothers were granted luxurious guest rooms within the palace."

King Leopold works on behalf of the best interests of his kingdom. The evidence is in this sentence: "The king, being the civilized man he was, did not want to execute the three brothers nor did he want to teach the civilians that it was fine to destroy Norman."

The Fox and the Cat

Ladder Set B

B1. Answers will vary. Some examples might include: running from his enemies, hiding, chasing the enemies, using a weapon, using martial arts, or distracting his enemies.

B2. Answers will vary. Some example categories based on the list above might include: escape by physical outmaneuvering, escape by tactical outmaneuvering, or escape by stealth.

B3. Answers will vary. An example based on the list and categories above might be: "One tried-and-true, good way of escape is better than multiple mediocre options."

Ladder Set C

C1.:

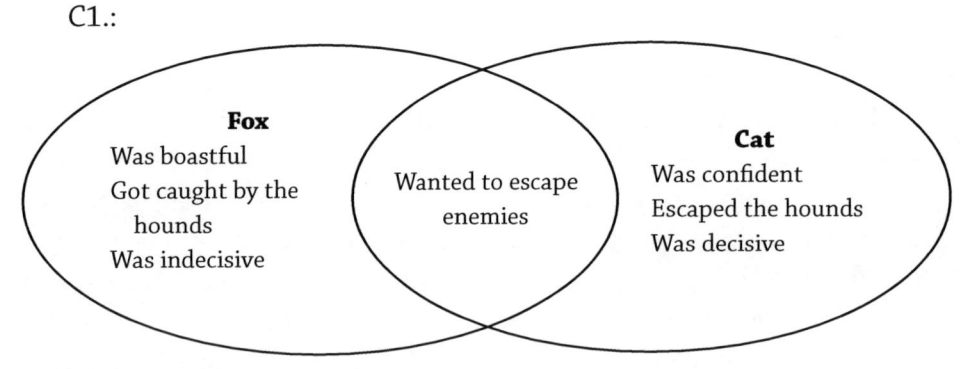

Fox
Was boastful
Got caught by the hounds
Was indecisive

Wanted to escape enemies

Cat
Was confident
Escaped the hounds
Was decisive

C2. The fox would be the kind of person who always talks about everything he can do, but when an actual situation arises he is unable to do anything at all. The cat would be the kind of person who doesn't say much but always comes through in a crucial situation. The evidence in the text to support my inferences are the fox's and the cat's words at the beginning of the fable, as well as the fact that the fox got caught and the cat did not.

C3.:

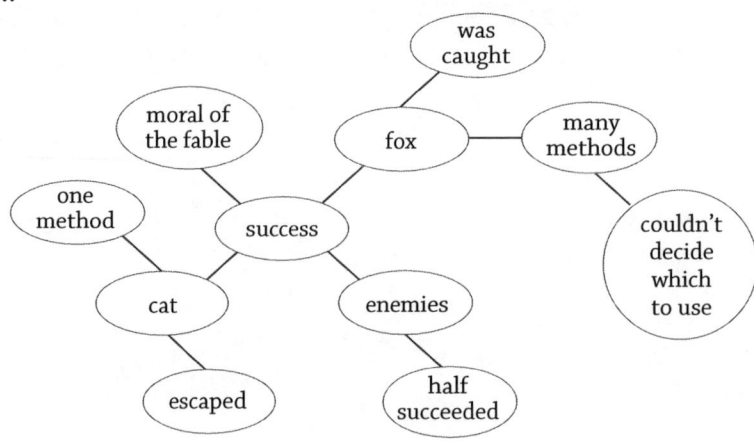

- moral of the fable
  - one method
    - cat
      - escaped
  - success
    - fox
      - was caught
      - many methods
        - couldn't decide which to use
    - enemies
      - half succeeded

The Lost Wig

Ladder Set A

A1. 1. The lion, who was wearing a wig, was walking down the street; 2. The lion saw a pretty tiger; 3. The lion bowed to the tiger; 4. The lion's wig flew off; 5. The lion made a funny comment rather than being embarrassed.

A2. The lion bowed because he was trying to make a good impression on the tiger. The effect of his action was for his wig to fly off and the tiger to know that he did not have a real mane.

A3. I think the tiger will laugh and begin a conversation with the lion. I think this will happen because the lion did not run off embarrassed, but instead acknowledged what happened with his wig. His comment let the lady tiger know that he did not take himself too seriously.

Ladder Set C

C1. Answers will vary. Students should include both physical and personality characteristics of the lion. His most important characteristics might include being able to laugh at himself because he did not get upset when his wig flew off; being vain and feeling he had to wear a wig in the first place; and wanting the lady tiger to like him because this desire caused him to bow, which led to his wig being blown off by the wind

C2. He expected the lady tiger to be flattered and impressed by his manners. The text says he wanted to "make an impression," and by smiling and bowing it can be inferred that he wanted to make a good impression.

C3. Answers will vary. An example might be, "Don't take your appearance too seriously." If the lion had gotten upset instead of making a joke about the way he looked without his wig, the atmosphere between the lion and the tiger would have been awkward.

Finding the Writer Inside

Ladder Set C

C1. In this story, the author is telling a story about Reed from Reed's perspective. She used dialogue to reveal more about Reed. For example, she wrote:

- "Mmmm-hmmmm," I mumbled, chewing my sandwich.
- "I didn't write anything," I mumbled again.
- "I didn't write anything, OK! You know how horrible I am at creative writing, I couldn't come up with any good ideas! Now stop bugging me about it!"

By including this sequence of comments in dialogue, you can understand her frustration with writing.

C2. The narrator seems to have problems getting started with her writing. The evidence that supports this is when she writes things like:
- "You know how horrible I am at creative writing, I couldn't come up with any good ideas!"
- "The next day, I was dreading English."
- "For a million years, I just sat there. Same thing as yesterday. All over again."

The inferences that you can make are that writing is hard for the narrator and that she is afraid when she gets a new writing assignment, so she can't write anything.

C3. The author might have shared this story with the world to show that even a reluctant writer can do a good job with writing. She wants to share these ideas like these:
- Sometimes writing is hard.
- It is sometimes hard to get started on challenging tasks.
- Encouragement from someone can help to motivate a person.

Ladder Set D

D1. The narrator decided it wouldn't work and folded up her paper. She felt dumb writing about mermaids in sixth grade. She also felt she wasn't good at creative writing and wondered if she would pass her unit. She also wondered why she had so much trouble writing when nobody else struggled.

D2. Completing a task with which one has difficulty requires persistence. Encouragement from someone may help to motivate a person to complete such a task.

D3. Answers will vary. Students should use the story as a model. They should include information that relates to the main idea of uneasiness in completing a certain task and how encouragement from someone may help to motivate a person.

The Myth of Athena

Ladder Set A

A1. 1. Zeus was threatened by the possibility of being overthrown by his child; 2. Zeus swallowed his pregnant wife, Metis; 3. Athena emerged from Zeus's split skull; 4. Athena became the goddess of wisdom and the goddess of war; 5. Athena was revered by the Greeks and was attributed with providing mankind all of the necessary knowledge for a civilization.

A2. Athena had so much wisdom because she possessed the combined wisdom of Zeus and Metis. When Zeus swallowed Metis, he absorbed her wisdom and combined it with his own. When Athena emerged from Zeus's skull, after Zeus had had a terrible headache, she had "inherited" the wisdom of both her parents.

A3. **Wagon:** We would not have transportation today. The wagon preceded the car as a mode of transportation. If mankind had never realized the increased efficiency of moving goods with a wagon compared to on foot, then we would all still be transporting goods by foot.

Plough: We would have more difficulty providing enough food for the world's population. The plough made farming faster and easier, thereby making it possible for one farmer to produce more crops and provide more food to more people.

Shipbuilding: We would not know anything about the rest of the world. America would probably have not been found. Ships enabled explorers and traders to sail to far away lands. Without ships we would only be able to explore areas that were connected by land.

Ladder Set D

D1. Athena was revered by the Greeks for her knowledge about how to advance mankind and make civilizations more efficient, as well as for her ability to plan war strategies, which led to successful outcomes for the Greeks.

D2. Athena's wisdom would have helped her as the goddess of war because she would have immense knowledge about different types of wars, tactics, and strategies. She also would be better able to understand the motives of the enemies through her knowledge of people.

D3. Answers will vary. Stories should refer to wisdom or knowledge about strategy or tactics as it applies to the winning of a war or series of wars.

The Myth of Heracles (Hercules)

Ladder Set A

A1. 1. Heracles strangled two serpents in his crib; 2. Heracles killed his children in an anger-induced frenzy; 3. Heracles was sentenced to complete 12 labors to atone for his wrongdoing; 4. He completed all of the labors without being harmed; 5. Heracles died from wearing a tunic tainted by poison.

A2. Heracles had to complete the 12 labors because he killed his children. He spent nearly his entire life completing the tasks; he did not get to spend time with his wife or use his strength to support his family. The labors were all-consuming.

A3. Heracles's manner of death was ironic because he had survived many more incidences that were far more dangerous than getting dressed. He did not know the tunic was full of poison because he could not see it. Therefore, he could defeat the enemies he could see, but not those that were disguised.

Ladder Set D

D1. Answers will vary. One may include: Heracles was forced to fight one of the most dangerous mythological creatures ever to have lived—the Hydra. The Hydra had many different heads that would regrow and double if they were cut off. If any of Hydra's heads were to breathe on Heracles, he would have died instantly. However, Heracles figured out the Hydra's heads could not grow back if the he was able to burn the wound he inflicted on the Hydra immediately after cutting off one of its heads. Heracles asked his nephew to help him; together they defeated the mighty Hydra.

D2. Heracles, who possessed superhuman strength, was able to defeat a series of mythical creatures and complete a series of arduous tasks to atone for the murder of his children. Nearly his whole life was spent in the completion of these tasks. Ironically, he died from an action much less dangerous than many he had completed before.

D3. Answers will vary. Students should include all of the elements of a myth, such as a god or goddess and a lesson to be learned. The character in the students' myths should have to atone for some crime he or she committed.

Theseus and the Minotaur

Ladder Set B

B1. Answers will vary. Some examples related to the story might include: by taking the place of the woman's son; by trusting Ariadne's directions regarding the labyrinth; by attacking the Minotaur; by going into the Labyrinth alone; by escaping King Minos's men; by not going back for Ariadne.

B2. Answers will vary. Some categories based on the above examples might be physical bravery, emotional bravery, and desire to help others.

B3. Answers will vary. An example based on the above categories and list might be, "Bravery is not just about doing dangerous physical actions."

Ladder Set D

D1. While Theseus was on Crete, he was in a hurry to find and slay the Minotaur without King Minos figuring out what he was doing. The beautiful daughter of King Minos, Ariadne, helped him by telling him the secrets of the labyrinth and giving him some gold thread to trail behind him. Theseus trusted Ariadne, even though he didn't know her very well. He found the Minotaur, killed it, and then found his way out of the labyrinth by following the trail of gold thread. Then, he rushed to his ship to get away from Crete before King Minos's soldiers could catch him.

D2. King Minos was mistreating the young people of Athens, and Theseus thought the cruelty should stop. As heir to the throne, Theseus decided it was his responsibility to rid Athens of the Minotaur menace. He killed the Minotaur and escaped King Minos's men. But, in the excitement of the moment, Theseus forgot to change his black sail to a white sail, which caused his father to jump off a cliff in grief for his lost son. Theseus won the respect of Athens and the love of Ariadne, but he lost his father.

D3. Answers will vary. Myth should be told from the point of view of one of the characters and should include all of the major events, such as Theseus taking the place of the boy, slaying the Minotaur, and escaping King Minos's men.

Poetry

These are suggested answers only. Answers will vary.

I Am Autumn

Ladder Set C

C1. There are many examples of personification in this poem. First of all, the poem is written from the point of view of autumn, because it is called "I Am Autumn." Throughout the poem, autumn does things that humans would do, such as shaking hands, dipping its finger in the snoozing lakes, and twirling its hair.

C2. Students may infer that the author feels that autumn is powerful and hurtful to things in nature. Students may cite many phrases such as these to support their inferences:
- "the poppies / They wilt at the sight of my glare"
- "I sentence death to the fields of green"
- "I will continue to weave / The blanket of frigid death"

C3. The titles will vary. There should be an acceptable explanation for the choice such as "These are all poems that are related to a specific season," or "These are all poems that portray a season in a specific way." The poem titles will reflect the generalization the student makes to explain his or her choices.

Ladder Set C

C1. Answers will vary, but should mention the way in which autumn does harmful things to plants and animals.

C2. Students should infer that autumn is mean and harmful to animals and plants. There are many examples, such as:
- "I sentence death to the fields of green"
- "I dip my finger in the snoozing lakes"
- "Freezing their lazy countenance"
- "I poke the bears into their dens"
- "And call out the snow owls"

C3. Answers will vary, although each poem should begin: "I Am _____ (name of a season)" and should continue for 12 lines. The poem should include examples of personification.

13 Ways of Looking at a Rose

Ladder Set B

B1. Each student should list characteristics that include: flirtatious, has deplorable petals, excitement when a bud, has beauty when it blooms, helps to brighten a room, rose stands up to bad weather, rose makes things seem sweeter, roses can keep people company, roses can be put together to make other things, and roses can flavor tea.

B2. The list should be sorted and classified by a system that the student can defend. Answers will vary but might include groups such as:
- What a rose looks like: has deplorable petals, has beauty when it blooms;
- How a rose helps: helps to brighten a room, rose makes things seem sweeter, roses can keep people company, roses can be put together to make other things, and roses can flavor tea;
- How a rose acts: flirtatious, causes excitement when a bud, has beauty when it blooms, rose stands up to bad weather; and so on.

B3. Answers will vary but should use the titles from the groups in B2. Examples might be: A rose looks a certain way; A rose can help people; A rose acts in certain ways; and so on.

Ladder Set C

C1. Examples of personification from the poem are: flirtatious roses, the rose stood fighting against the wind, the roses stand in a line, and so on.

C2. Answers will vary; the students should infer that the author seems to like the rose and is interested in its qualities. They should be able to explain reasons for these feelings, using evidence from the poem. For example, "The narrator seems to like the rose. She says 'it is held in a man's hand to make a perfect moment.'"

C3. Answers will vary. Each student should create a poem that is at least 16 lines long about multiple ways of looking at something else.

Sweet Summer

Ladder Set B

B1. Characteristics should include: has brambles and thorns, makes a person's hands sticky, causes red and purple stains, bumpy, squishy, and so on.

B2. The answers can be sorted in any logical way. This is an example:

Sight	Sound	Feel	Taste
Causes red and purple stains	Softly plunk	Has brambles and thorns	Sweet
Perfect one	Birds chirp nearby	Hairs tickling my tongue	Sour
	Bumblebees hum nearby	Bumpy	
		Squishy	

B3. Students should examine their categories from B2 and make generalizations about adjectives, such as the following: descriptive words help the reader better understand what the author is writing about, and descriptive words help the author create a word picture for the reader. When people picture things in their minds they might be able to better understand the reading. For the second question, students should conclude that there is a balance of using too many or too few adjectives. Writers need to include enough descriptive words to help the reader create images in his or her mind, but using too many may confuse the reader or make the reader lose track of the important points in the story.

Ladder Set C

C1. Examples of personification may include the "brambles and thorns claw my arms"; "hairs tickling my tongue"; and so on.

C2. Answers may vary, but may include:
- "Reaching in, brambles and thorns claw my arms": It has sharp parts.

- "birds chirp on nearby bushes and bumblebees hum softly": Animals are attracted to it.
- "Plucking with sticky red and purple stained hands": The color of the blackberry is a combination of red and purple.
- "softly plunking into my almost full bucket": It is not heavy but is dense enough to make a sound.
- "The sweet and sour sensation with hairs tickling my tongue": It is a fruit with a textured skin.
- "The perfect one, just out of reach": They vary in their appearance.
- "leaning, stretching out my arm": A person may have to reach in the branches to get a good one.
- "I feel the bumpy, squishy fruit on my fingertips": The texture is not smooth; the object is soft.
- "Just then, it drops out of sight in the thick brambles": It can be easily concealed by the branches on which it grows.
- "There goes my perfect blackberry."

C3. Answers will vary; students should select an object, brainstorm ways to describe that object, and use those brainstormed words in a poem similar to "Sweet Summer." Look for personification in their poems. Prior to having students write their own personification poems, you may need to work with the entire class to brainstorm ways to personify an object.

My Shadow

Ladder Set B

B1. Answers will vary, but might include: like the little boy; likes to grow; doesn't know how to play; cowardly; lazy

B2. Answers will vary. Students should create lists of the words and phrases from activity 1 and create a title for each list.

B3. Answers will vary, but might include: shadows do whatever the person does; shadows don't know how to play.

Ladder Set C

C1. He describes his shadow as a friend, but an annoying friend.

C2.:

Like the little boy (narrator)	Unlike other children
Jumps	Not like a regular child in how he grows
Grows quickly	Doesn't know how children should play
Stays too close	Makes fun of the narrator
Sleepy head	Not brave

C3. Answers will vary. The author wants the reader to know that a child can have a playmate and be creative even when he is alone.

After the Winter

Ladder Set B

B1. Answers will vary. Students will list words and phrases that are used to describe the time of year that comes after the winter. Their lists might include the following:
- "summer isle"
- "Where bamboos spire to shafted grove"
- "orchids smile"
- "laughing crystal rill"
- "droning bee"
- "blue-bells blowing near"

B2. Answers will vary. The student will categorize their phrases describing the time that comes after winter and label each category with a describing word.

B3. Answers will vary. Students may generalize that the time after winter is hopeful. The time after winter allows everything to have a new start in life. They also may note that the time after winter is represented by positive images.

Ladder Set C

C1. Personification appears in the following phrases:
- "bamboos spire to shafted grove"
- "wide-mouthed orchids smile"
- "towers the cotton tree"
- "leaps the laughing crystal rill"

C2. Answers will vary. Students should explain their choice and use evidence from the poem to explain their answer.

C3. Answers will vary. The author is trying to show that there is always hope for a new start in life, even after a tough time.

Travel

Ladder Set B

B1. Answers will vary. The narrator likes traveling. The narrator views the train as her means for travel; she associates any train with her love of traveling. The narrator enjoys meeting people when she travels.

B2. Answers will vary. Some students may infer that the narrator yearns to travel. They may also infer that she has not had the opportunities to travel that she wishes she had.

B3. Answers will vary. Students should make two generalizations. Example: The narrator loves traveling. The narrator loves meeting new people when she travels.

Ladder Set C

C1. The images you can see from reading this poem are: loud voices speaking; a still, quiet night; red cinders flying out from a train; the sound of a steam engine; the warmth ones feels when spending time with friends.

C2. Answers will vary. Students may say that the poem conveys the author's desire for adventure; even though she is content with her life, when she hears the train she thinks of other possibilities for her life. Examples of words from the poem might be: "there isn't a train goes by all day / But I hear its whistle shrieking" and "Though the night is still for sleep and dreaming, / But I see its cinders red on the sky, / And hear its engine steaming." An author carefully chooses words to create a certain mood.

C3. Answers will vary. Students may say that the author has a strong desire to travel. The theme of the poem is that travel is a way to have new adventures and meet new people. She uses the train as a symbol for this.

Saving Words

Ladder Set C

A1.:
1. The teacher tells students to write a poem.
2. The narrator struggles to figure out what to write.
3. The narrator writes a poem.
4. The poem is lost, because it did not transmit and get saved on the computer.

A2. Diagrams will vary. See the poem for evidence. Possible effects could include: getting in trouble for not submitting work; getting a low grade for not submitting work; being upset because he worked hard and lost his poem after he had finally written something; and so on.

A3. Student poems will vary. Make sure the students write about a situation when something has been problematic for them, because they made a mistake or due to the fault of something else.

Ladder Set C

C1. The author using rhyming words in this poem. Each set of two lines has rhyming words.

C2. By "The poem comes pouring out, literary mastery," the author is saying that he was suddenly able to write a good poem easily.

C3. Letters will vary. Students' work should include details regarding why the author did not submit a poem.

Dubstep

Ladder Set B

B1. Words or phrases that relate to music include:
- "the perfect song"
- "The beats start building up"
- "Electrical music's stirring up"
- "The rhythm gets louder and louder"
- "the music goes completely still"
- "you hear the song go"
- "intensity of the beat starts to grow"
- "the bass goes loud"
- "the notes stretch out"
- "best song without a doubt"
- "music begins to calm its way down"
- "sounds get loud with a steady fast thump"
- "notes hitting hard"
- "rhythm's appealing"
- "music slows down and starts to flow"
- "last notes are sounding"

B2. Answers will vary. Students should put the answers from Activity B1 into categories and make appropriate titles for each group.

B3. Answers will vary. Students should write three generalizations about their categories from Activity B2.

Ladder Set C

C1. Examples of onomatopoeia include:
- "DUB-WUB"
- "BOOM-BANG the bass goes loud"
- "WUB-WUB the notes stretch out"
- "DUB-WUB-CRASH"
- "BOOM-BANG-PANG"
- "WUB-WUB-BUB"

C2. Answers will vary. The last words in each set of two lines rhyme with each other. The author was trying to create a beat within the poem to mimic the beat in dubstep music. The author wants the reader to appreciate dubstep; he uses words and phrases like "this rhythm's appealing," "dubstep makes you feel like a pro," and "the masterpiece."

C3. Answers will vary. The author seems to think that dubstep is a good type of music.

Approach of Winter

Ladder Set B

B1. Answers will vary. Students will chose an object and list human characteristics for the object.

B2. Answers will vary. Students will create two T-charts. They will use one to list phrases from the poem and characteristics of leaves that may have prompted the author to use those phrases. They will use the other T-chart to list phrases they created in Activity B1 and characteristics of the real object that prompted them to use those phrases.

B3. Answers will vary. Be sure students apply the generalization appropriately in their paragraphs.

Ladder Set C

C1. Human characteristics the author gave the leaves are: "refuse to let go" and "stream bitterly out to one side."

C2. The author thinks that the approaching winter is harsh. He uses words like: "half-stripped," "struck by a wind," "flutter drily," "driven like hail," "bare garden," and so on.

C3. Answers will vary.

Nonfiction

These are suggested answers only. Answers will vary.

The American Revolution

Ladder Set C

C1. Answers will vary. Check students' answers for consistency with the type of colonist they choose. For example, if they choose to write from the point of view of a Patriot, then the description of the character should include support of the war.

C2. Answers will vary. Possible answers might include: the French became allies with the Americans because they wanted another chance to fight Britain; they disliked Britain so much that they would ally themselves with anyone who was fighting against Britain; they supported freedom for America; and so forth.

C3. Answers will vary. Possible answers might include: liberty, freedom, independence, right to form their own government, democracy, and so forth.

Ladder Set D

D1. Answers will vary. Students must restate the quotations and not merely change a few words.

D2. Answers will vary. Students should include important events such as taxation without representation, the Boston Massacre, the desire for a democratic government, and so forth.

D3. Answers will vary. Check students' answers for consistency and accuracy with respect to their chosen point of view.

The Exploration of Space

Ladder Set A

A1. Oct. 4, 1957, Soviet Union launched Sputnik; April 12, 1961, Yuri Gagarin, Soviet cosmonaut, became the first human to travel into space; December 1968, Apollo 8 orbited the moon 10 times; July 20, 1969, Neil Armstrong became the first astronaut to walk on the moon

A2. When the space shuttle is launching, the Earth's gravitational pull makes it difficult for the spacecraft to move. The spacecraft must use a lot of rocket-fueled power to break the pull of gravity. After the spacecraft reenters the atmosphere, Earth's gravitational pull causes it to start falling back to Earth.

A3. Answers will vary. Students should mention that space exploration has allowed scientists to learn a lot about the universe beyond Earth. They also should provide examples from the text and/or from prior knowledge.

Ladder Set D

D1. Answers will vary. Students must restate the quotation, not merely change a few words.

D2. Answers will vary. Students should include the important elements of space exploration, such as manned shuttles, satellites, robots, and SAFER.

D3. Answers will vary. Evaluate student responses based on creativity, specificity, and accuracy.

Graphic Ice Cream

Ladder Set B

B1. Answers will vary. Check students' answers to ensure they are accurate in terms of listing data that can be collected. Examples include: classmates' favorite books, rainfall, snowfall, grades on tests, number of students buying lunch each day, growth rate of plants, and so forth.

B2. Answers will vary based on details on students' lists. Details in each category should match the definitions of bar, line, and pie graphs found in the text.

B3. Answers will vary. Generalizations should be broad, overarching statements about the use of graphs to represent data.

Ladder Set C

C1. Answers will vary. Possible answers might include: responsible; eager to make their business as efficient as possible; good managers; interested in making money; considerate of their customers; and so forth.

C2. Answers will vary. Possible answers might include:
- The customers' favorite flavor is strawberry cheesecake; their least favorite flavor is vanilla; they should stock plenty of strawberries and pecans.
- The day with the most customers is Friday; the day with the least customers is Sunday; the owners might be losing money by staying open on Sunday.
- The employees spend most of their time preparing orders; they spend the least amount of time reconciling the register; and the employees are good workers who use their time wisely.

C3. Answers will vary. Students should include a statement about graphs being a description of the kind of data used by the ice cream store owners to analyze the efficiency and effectiveness of their business.

The Great Depression

Ladder Set A

A1. Stock market crash of 1929; drought in the Midwest during the summer of 1930; unemployment in 1930 and 1931; inauguration of FDR in 1933; downturn in the economy in 1937; beginning of WWII in 1939; upswing in European economies from 1937–1939; end of the Great Depression/U.S. enters WWII in 1941.

A2. The end of the Great Depression in Europe was caused by the re-armament of troops to protect the world against Nazi Germany; the end of the Great Depression in America was caused by the creation of jobs to produce large amounts of war supplies and rations to support the war effort as the U.S. began fighting in WWII.

A3. Answers will vary. Possible answers might include: They couldn't go to school to get an education, which would lead to better jobs in the future; they did not have homes to live in and therefore did not enjoy the security that children today experience; they were often hungry and malnourished; they may not have grown as well as they should because they didn't have enough to eat and may, therefore, have shortened life spans; they may have psychological trauma that affects their lives even today; and so forth.

Ladder Set B

B1. Answers will vary. Check students' answers for relevance and accuracy.

B2. Answers will vary based on the details on their list. Make sure students' categories make sense and are logically organized.

B3. Answers will vary. Generalizations should be broad, overarching statements about the differences between their lives as children today compared to life as a child during the Great Depression.

It's Electric!

Ladder Set B

B1. Answers will vary. Check students' lists to ensure they include examples of the use of electricity only.

B2. Answers will vary. Students should group details into logical categories without using a "miscellaneous" or "other" category.

B3. Answers will vary. Generalizations should be broad, overarching statements about the use of electricity.

Ladder Set D

D1. Answers will vary. Students should restate the quotation in their own words and not merely make minor changes to the statement. For example, a possible response might be: "Electricity will be so common that only people who have time and money to waste will spend it on using candles."

D2. Answers will vary. Students should include the important elements of static electricity, including charges build up, opposite charges attract, like charges repel, and overcharged objects will transfer charged particles to neutral objects.

D3. Answers will vary. Check students' answers for originality and audience appeal.

The Metric System vs. the U.S. Customary System

Ladder Set A

A1. *Metric system*: origin, goals, measurement of length, liquid, weight; prefixes; lack of conversion factors; time

U.S. Customary system: origin, the U.S. is the only country that hasn't converted; Omnibus Trade and Competitiveness Act of 1988; measurement of length, general volume, liquid volume, and weight; conversion factors; chart comparing conversion

A2. The French adopted the metric system because they wanted a standard, single unit to measure physical quantity without the need for conversion factors and with a common set of prefixes.

A3. Answers will vary. Possible answers may include: trade with foreign countries will become more difficult for the United States; the United States believes it does not have to conform to what the rest of the world is doing; the United States likes being different; it would be too difficult to change the entire nation to the metric system because most everyone learns the customary system in school; and so forth.

Ladder Set C

C1. Answers will vary. Students should clearly support the metric or the customary system. Check their answers for cohesion, logic, and supporting details.

C2. Answers will vary. Possible answers might include: The metric system is easier to convert between units; the customary system has units of measurement that are easier to pronounce and remember; the metric system is more organized and logical; the customary system has significantly different names for different measurement units that make it less confusing.

C3. Answers will vary. Check students' answers for justification through relevant supporting details.

Common Core State Standards Alignment

Cluster	Common Core State Standards in ELA-Literacy
College and Career Readiness Anchor Standards for Reading	CCRA.R.1 Read closely to determine what the text says explicitly and to make logical inferences from it; cite specific textual evidence when writing or speaking to support conclusions drawn from the text. (Short Stories: Ladders A, B, C) (Poetry: Ladders A, B, C) (Nonfiction: Ladders A, B, C, D)
	CCRA.R.2 Determine central ideas or themes of a text and analyze their development; summarize the key supporting details and ideas. (Short Stories: Ladders A, B, C, D) (Poetry: Ladders A, B, C, D) (Nonfiction: Ladders A, B, C, D)
	CCRA.R.3 Analyze how and why individuals, events, or ideas develop and interact over the course of a text. (Short Stories: Ladders A, B, C) (Poetry: Ladders A, B) (Nonfiction: Ladders A, B, C, D)
	CCRA.R.4 Interpret words and phrases as they are used in a text, including determining technical, connotative, and figurative meanings, and analyze how specific word choices shape meaning or tone. (Short Stories: Ladder C) (Poetry: Ladders C, D)
	CCRA.R.5 Analyze the structure of texts, including how specific sentences, paragraphs, and larger portions of the text (e.g., a section, chapter, scene, or stanza) relate to each other and the whole. (Poetry: Ladder B)
	CCRA.R.6 Assess how point of view or purpose shapes the content and style of a text. (Short Stories: Ladders B, D) (Poetry: Ladder C) (Nonfiction: Ladder C)

Cluster	Common Core State Standards in ELA-Literacy
College and Career Readiness Anchor Standards for Reading, *continued*	CCRA.R.10 Read and comprehend complex literary and informational texts independently and proficiently. (Short Stories: Ladders A, B, C, D) (Poetry: Ladders A, B, C, D) (Nonfiction: Ladders A, B, C, D)
College and Career Readiness Anchor Standards for Writing	CCRA.W.2 Write informative/explanatory texts to examine and convey complex ideas and information clearly and accurately through the effective selection, organization, and analysis of content. (Short Stories: Ladders B, C, D) (Poetry: Ladders B, C, D) (Nonfiction: Ladders A, B, D)
	CCRA.W.3 Write narratives to develop real or imagined experiences or events using effective technique, well-chosen details and well-structured event sequences. (Short Stories: Ladder D) (Poetry: Ladders A, C, D) (Nonfiction: Ladder D)
	CCRA.W.9 Draw evidence from literary or informational texts to support analysis, reflection, and research. (Short Stories: Ladders B, C, D) (Poetry: Ladders A, B, C, D) (Nonfiction: Ladders A, B, D)
College and Career Readiness Anchor Standards for Speaking and Listening	CCRA.SL.1 Prepare for and participate effectively in a range of conversations and collaborations with diverse partners, building on others' ideas and expressing their own clearly and persuasively. (Short Stories: Ladders A, B, C, D) (Poetry: Ladders A, B, C, D) (Nonfiction: Ladders A, B, C, D)
	CCRA.SL.4 Present information, findings, and supporting evidence such that listeners can follow the line of reasoning and the organization, development, and style are appropriate to task, purpose, and audience. (Short Stories: Ladders A, B, C, D) (Poetry: Ladders A, B, C, D) (Nonfiction: Ladders A, B, C, D)
	CCRA.SL.6 Adapt speech to a variety of contexts and communicative tasks, demonstrating command of formal English when indicated or appropriate. (Short Stories: Ladders A, B, C, D) (Poetry: Ladders A, B, C, D) (Nonfiction: Ladders A, B, C, D)
College and Career Readiness Anchor Standards for Language	CCRA.L.1 Demonstrate command of the conventions of standard English grammar and usage when writing or speaking. (Short Stories: Ladders A, B, C, D) (Poetry: Ladders A, B, C, D) (Nonfiction: Ladders A, B, C, D)
	CCRA.L.3 Apply knowledge of language to understand how language functions in different contexts, to make effective choices for meaning or style, and to comprehend more fully when reading or listening. (Short Stories: Ladders A, B, C, D) (Poetry: Ladders A, B, C, D) (Nonfiction: Ladders A, B, C, D)
	CCRA.L.5 Demonstrate understanding of figurative language, word relationships, and nuances in word meanings. (Poetry: Ladders C, D)

Cluster	Common Core State Standards in ELA-Literacy
Reading: Literature, Grade 4	RL.4.1 Refer to details and examples in a text when explaining what the text says explicitly and when drawing inferences from the text. (Short Stories: Ladders A, B, C) (Poetry: Ladders A, B, C)
	RL.4.2 Determine a theme of a story, drama, or poem from details in the text; summarize the text. (Short Stories: Ladders A, B, C, D) (Poetry: Ladders A, B, C, D)
	RL.4.3 Describe in depth a character, setting, or event in a story or drama, drawing on specific details in the text (e.g., a character's thoughts, words, or actions). (Short Stories: Ladders A, B, C) (Poetry: Ladders A, B, C)
	RL.4.4 Determine the meaning of words and phrases as they are used in a text, including those that allude to significant characters found in mythology (e.g., Herculean). (Short Stories: Ladder C) (Poetry: Ladders C, D)
	RL.4.10 By the end of the year, read and comprehend literature, including stories, dramas, and poetry, in the grades 4–5 text complexity band proficiently, with scaffolding as needed at the high end of the range. (Short Stories: Ladders A,C) (Poetry: Ladder A)
Reading: Literature, Grade 5	RL.5.1 Quote accurately from a text when explaining what the text says explicitly and when drawing inferences from the text. (Short Stories: Ladders A, B, C) (Poetry: Ladders A, B, C)
	RL.5.2 Determine a theme of a story, drama, or poem from details in the text, including how characters in a story or drama respond to challenges or how the speaker in a poem reflects upon a topic; summarize the text. (Short Stories: Ladders A, B, C, D) (Poetry: Ladders A, B, C, D)
	RL.5.3 Compare and contrast two or more characters, settings, or events in a story or drama, drawing on specific details in the text (e.g., how characters interact). (Short Stories: Ladders B, C) (Poetry: Ladders B, C)
	RL.5.4 Determine the meaning of words and phrases as they are used in a text, including figurative language such as metaphors and similes. (Short Stories: Ladder C) (Poetry: Ladders C, D)
	RL.5.10 By the end of the year, read and comprehend literature, including stories, dramas, and poetry, at the high end of the grades 4–5 text complexity band independently and proficiently. (Short Stories: Ladders A, B, C, D) (Poetry: Ladders A, B, C, D)

Cluster	Common Core State Standards in ELA-Literacy
Reading: Literature, Grade 6	RL.6.1 Cite textual evidence to support analysis of what the text says explicitly as well as inferences drawn from the text. (Short Stories: Ladders A, B, C) (Poetry: Ladders A, B, C)
	RL.6.2 Determine a theme or central idea of a text and how it is conveyed through particular details; provide a summary of the text distinct from personal opinions or judgments.(Short Stories: Ladders A, B, C, D) (Poetry: Ladders A, B, C, D)
	RL.6.3 Describe how a particular story's or drama's plot unfolds in a series of episodes as well as how the characters respond or change as the plot moves toward a resolution. (Short Stories: Ladders A, B, C, D) (Poetry: Ladders A, B)
	RL.6.4 Determine the meaning of words and phrases as they are used in a text, including figurative and connotative meanings; analyze the impact of a specific word choice on meaning and tone. (Short Stories: Ladder C) (Poetry: Ladders C, D)
	RL.6.10 By the end of the year, read and comprehend literature, including stories, dramas, and poems, in the grades 6–8 text complexity band proficiently, with scaffolding as needed at the high end of the range. (Short Stories: Ladders A, B, C, D) (Poetry: Ladders A, B, C, D)
Reading: Informational Text: Grade 4	RI.4.1 Refer to details and examples in a text when explaining what the text says explicitly and when drawing inferences from the text. (Nonfiction: Ladders A, B, C, D)
	RI.4.2 Determine the main idea of a text and explain how it is supported by key details; summarize the text. (Nonfiction: Ladders A, B, C, D)
	RI.4.3 Explain events, procedures, ideas, or concepts in a historical, scientific, or technical text, including what happened and why, based on specific information in the text. (Nonfiction: Ladders A, C, D)
	RI.4.4 Determine the meaning of general academic and domain-specific words or phrases in a text relevant to a grade 4 topic or subject area. (Nonfiction: Ladders A, B, C, D)
	RI.4.5 Describe the overall structure (e.g., chronology, comparison, cause/effect, problem/solution) of events, ideas, concepts, or information in a text or part of a text. (Nonfiction: Ladder A)
	RI.4.7 Interpret information presented visually, orally, or quantitatively (e.g., in charts, graphs, diagrams, time lines, animations, or interactive elements on Web pages) and explain how the information contributes to an understanding of the text in which it appears. (Nonfiction: Ladders B, C)

Cluster	Common Core State Standards in ELA-Literacy
Reading: Informational Text: Grade 4, *continued*	RI.4.10 By the end of year, read and comprehend informational texts, including history/social studies, science, and technical texts, in the grades 4–5 text complexity band proficiently, with scaffolding as needed at the high end of the range. (Nonfiction: Ladders A, B, C, D)
Reading: Informational Text: Grade 5	RI.5.1 Quote accurately from a text when explaining what the text says explicitly and when drawing inferences from the text. (Nonfiction: Ladders A, B, C, D)
	RI.5.2 Determine two or more main ideas of a text and explain how they are supported by key details; summarize the text. (Nonfiction: Ladders A, B, D)
	RI.5.3 Explain the relationships or interactions between two or more individuals, events, ideas, or concepts in a historical, scientific, or technical text based on specific information in the text. (Nonfiction: Ladders A, C, D)
	RI.5.4 Determine the meaning of general academic and domain-specific words and phrases in a text relevant to a grade 5 topic or subject area. (Nonfiction: Ladders A, B, C, D)
	RI.5.5 Compare and contrast the overall structure (e.g., chronology, comparison, cause/effect, problem/solution) of events, ideas, concepts, or information in two or more texts. (Nonfiction: Ladder A)
	RI.5.10 By the end of the year, read and comprehend informational texts, including history/social studies, science, and technical texts, at the high end of the grades 4–5 text complexity band independently and proficiently. (Nonfiction: Ladders A, B, C, D)
Reading: Informational Text: Grade 6	RI.6.1 Cite textual evidence to support analysis of what the text says explicitly as well as inferences drawn from the text. (Nonfiction: Ladders A, B, C, D)
	RI.6.22 Determine a central idea of a text and how it is conveyed through particular details; provide a summary of the text distinct from personal opinions or judgments. (Nonfiction: Ladders A, B, C, D)
	RI.6.3 Analyze in detail how a key individual, event, or idea is introduced, illustrated, and elaborated in a text (e.g., through examples or anecdotes). (Nonfiction: Ladders A, C, D)
	RI.6.10 By the end of the year, read and comprehend literary nonfiction in the grades 6–8 text complexity band proficiently, with scaffolding as needed at the high end of the range. (Nonfiction: Ladders A, B, C, D)

Cluster	Common Core State Standards in ELA-Literacy
Writing, Grade 4	W.4.2 Write informative/explanatory texts to examine a topic and convey ideas and information clearly. (Short Stories: Ladders B, C, D) (Poetry: Ladders B, C, D) (Nonfiction: Ladders A, B, D)
	W.4.3 Write narratives to develop real or imagined experiences or events using effective technique, descriptive details, and clear event sequences. (Short Stories: Ladder D) (Poetry: Ladders A, C, D) (Nonfiction: Ladder D)
	W.4.9 Draw evidence from literary or informational texts to support analysis, reflection, and research. (Short Stories: Ladders B, C, D) (Poetry: Ladders A, B, C, D) (Nonfiction: Ladders A, B, D)
Writing, Grade 5	W.5.2 Write informative/explanatory texts to examine a topic and convey ideas and information clearly. (Short Stories: Ladders B, C, D) (Poetry: Ladders B, C, D) (Nonfiction: Ladders A, B, D)
	W.5.3 Write narratives to develop real or imagined experiences or events using effective technique, descriptive details, and clear event sequences. (Short Stories: Ladder D) (Poetry: Ladders A, C, D) (Nonfiction: Ladder D)
	W.5.9 Draw evidence from literary or informational texts to support analysis, reflection, and research. (Short Stories: Ladders B, C, D) (Poetry: Ladders A, B, C, D) (Nonfiction: Ladders A, B, D)
Writing, Grade 6	W.6.2 Write informative/explanatory texts to examine a topic and convey ideas, concepts, and information through the selection, organization, and analysis of relevant content. (Short Stories: Ladders B, C, D) (Poetry: Ladders B, C, D) (Nonfiction: Ladders A, B, D)
	W.6.3 Write narratives to develop real or imagined experiences or events using effective technique, relevant descriptive details, and well-structured event sequences. (Short Stories: Ladder D) (Poetry: Ladders A, C, D) (Nonfiction: Ladder D)
	W.6.9 Draw evidence from literary or informational texts to support analysis, reflection, and research. (Short Stories: Ladders B, C, D) (Poetry: Ladders A, B, C, D) (Nonfiction: Ladders A, B, D)
Speaking and Listening, Grade 4	SL.4.1 Engage effectively in a range of collaborative discussions (one-on-one, in groups, and teacher-led) with diverse partners on grade 4 topics and texts, building on others' ideas and expressing their own clearly. (Short Stories: Ladders A, B, C, D) (Poetry: Ladders A, B, C, D) (Nonfiction: Ladders A, B, C, D)

Cluster	Common Core State Standards in ELA-Literacy
Speaking and Listening, Grade 4, *continued*	SL.4.2 Paraphrase portions of a text read aloud or information presented in diverse media and formats, including visually, quantitatively, and orally. (Short Stories: Ladder D) (Poetry: Ladder D) (Nonfiction: Ladder D)
	SL.4.4 Report on a topic or text, tell a story, or recount an experience in an organized manner, using appropriate facts and relevant, descriptive details to support main ideas or themes; speak clearly at an understandable pace. (Short Stories: Ladders A, B, C, D) (Poetry: Ladders A, B, C, D) (Nonfiction: Ladders A, B, C, D)
Speaking and Listening, Grade 5	SL.5.1 Engage effectively in a range of collaborative discussions (one-on-one, in groups, and teacher-led) with diverse partners on grade 5 topics and texts, building on others' ideas and expressing their own clearly. (Short Stories: Ladders A, B, C, D) (Poetry: Ladders A, B, C, D) (Nonfiction: Ladders A, B, C, D)
	SL.5.2 Summarize a written text read aloud or information presented in diverse media and formats, including visually, quantitatively, and orally. (Short Stories: Ladder D) (Poetry: Ladder D) (Nonfiction: Ladder D)
	SL.5.4 Report on a topic or text or present an opinion, sequencing ideas logically and using appropriate facts and relevant, descriptive details to support main ideas or themes; speak clearly at an understandable pace. (Short Stories: Ladders A, B, C, D) (Poetry: Ladders A, B, C, D) (Nonfiction: Ladders A, B, C, D)
Speaking and Listening, Grade 6	SL.6.1 Engage effectively in a range of collaborative discussions (one-on-one, in groups, and teacher-led) with diverse partners on grade 6 topics, texts, and issues, building on others' ideas and expressing their own clearly. (Short Stories: Ladders A, B, C, D) (Poetry: Ladders A, B, C, D) (Nonfiction: Ladders A, B, C, D)
	SL.6.4 Present claims and findings, sequencing ideas logically and using pertinent descriptions, facts, and details to accentuate main ideas or themes; use appropriate eye contact, adequate volume, and clear pronunciation. (Short Stories: Ladders A, B, C, D) (Poetry: Ladders A, B, C, D) (Nonfiction: Ladders A, B, C, D)

Cluster	Common Core State Standards in ELA-Literacy
Language, Grade 4	L.4.1 Demonstrate command of the conventions of standard English grammar and usage when writing or speaking. (Short Stories: Ladders A, B, C, D) (Poetry: Ladders A, B, C, D) (Nonfiction: Ladders A, B, C, D)
	L.4.3 Use knowledge of language and its conventions when writing, speaking, reading, or listening. (Short Stories: Ladders A, B, C, D) (Poetry: Ladders A, B, C, D) (Nonfiction: Ladders A, B, C, D)
	L.4.5 Demonstrate understanding of figurative language, word relationships, and nuances in word meanings. (Poetry: Ladders C, D)
Language, Grade 5	L.5.1 Demonstrate command of the conventions of standard English grammar and usage when writing or speaking. (Short Stories: Ladders A, B, C, D) (Poetry: Ladders A, B, C, D) (Nonfiction: Ladders A, B, C, D)
	L.5.3 Use knowledge of language and its conventions when writing, speaking, reading, or listening. (Short Stories: Ladders A, B, C, D) (Poetry: Ladders A, B, C, D) (Nonfiction: Ladders A, B, C, D)
	L.5.5 Demonstrate understanding of figurative language, word relationships, and nuances in word meanings. (Poetry: Ladders C, D)
Language, Grade 6	L.6.1 Demonstrate command of the conventions of standard English grammar and usage when writing or speaking. (Short Stories: Ladders A, B, C, D) (Poetry: Ladders A, B, C, D) (Nonfiction: Ladders A, B, C, D)
	L.6.3 Use knowledge of language and its conventions when writing, speaking, reading, or listening. (Short Stories: Ladders A, B, C, D) (Poetry: Ladders A, B, C, D) (Nonfiction: Ladders A, B, C, D)
	L.6.5 Demonstrate understanding of figurative language, word relationships, and nuances in word meanings. (Poetry: Ladders C, D)
Literacy in History/ Social Studies, Grades 6-8	RH.6-8.1 Cite specific textual evidence to support analysis of primary and secondary sources. (Nonfiction: Ladders A, C, D)
	RH.6-8.2 Determine the central ideas or information of a primary or secondary source; provide an accurate summary of the source distinct from prior knowledge or opinions. (Nonfiction: Ladders B, C, D)
	RH.6-8.4 Determine the meaning of words and phrases as they are used in a text, including vocabulary specific to domains related to history/social studies. (Nonfiction: Ladders A, B, C, D)

Cluster	Common Core State Standards in ELA-Literacy
Literacy in History/ Social Studies, Grades 6-8, *continued*	RH.6-8.5 Describe how a text presents information (e.g., sequentially, comparatively, causally). (Nonfiction: Ladder A)
	RH.6-8.10 By the end of grade 8, read and comprehend history/social studies texts in the grades 6–8 text complexity band independently and proficiently. (Nonfiction: Ladders A, B, C, D)
Literacy in Science/Technical Subjects, Grades 6-8	RST.6-8.1 Cite specific textual evidence to support analysis of science and technical texts. (Nonfiction: Ladders A, C, D)
	RST.6-8.2 Determine the central ideas or conclusions of a text; provide an accurate summary of the text distinct from prior knowledge or opinions. (Nonfiction: Ladders B, C, D)
	RST.6-8.4 Determine the meaning of symbols, key terms, and other domain-specific words and phrases as they are used in a specific scientific or technical context relevant to grades 6–8 texts and topics. (Nonfiction: Ladders A, B, C, D)
	RST.6-8.5 Describe how a text presents information (e.g., sequentially, comparatively, causally). (Nonfiction: Ladder A)
	RST.6-8.10 By the end of grade 8, read and comprehend science/technical texts in the grades 6–8 text complexity band independently and proficiently. (Nonfiction: Ladders A, B, C, D)